"My prediction is that *The Selle.* timeless classic—an indispensable handbook guiding business owners through one of the most vexing chapters of their lives. Advisors who understand that a business owner's transition is more than a transaction will buy this book by the truckload and change the world one deal at a time."

—Thomas William Deans, PhD,
author of *Every Family's Business* and *Willing Wisdom*

"This book is a must read for both business owners and their advisors. It can help enhance the results realized and reduce the stress for all involved in the ownership transition process. Denise paints a vivid picture of the characters in this unique, easy-to-read story of a complex journey too few successfully complete. Having personally played more than one of these roles in my career, the array of traits, concerns and actions woven into the narrative vibrated between my ears. ... [Its] messages, when understood and applied, will dramatically improve any owner's journey to and through the successful sale their business."

—Richard Mowrey, #1 internationally best-selling
author of *When Is the Right Time to Sell My Business?*

"Denise provides a refreshing viewpoint on the human side of a business transition. This is a much-needed perspective in the transaction world. I felt like I was walking along side Marty. The nuggets of advice are invaluable. Her desire to change deal mentality is contagious!"

—Jennifer L. Todd,
Transaction Services Director, BSM Consulting

"Couldn't put it down ... *The Seller's Journey* explains the psychology behind an owner's emotional experience at the culmination of their life's work. A must-read for owners, buyers and the world of advisors involved in the process."

—Dr. Jamie Weiner, high-net-worth family advisor, author of *The Legacy Conversation*

"In *The Seller's Journey*, veteran advisor Denise Logan unravels the emotion-fueled obstacles to closing a sale and shows us how to resolve them. A must read for anyone involved in selling a company."

—Terri Tierney Clark, former private equity/ investment banking advisor, author of *Learn, Work, Lead—Things Your Mentor Won't Tell You*

Transition expert Denise Logan "offers the only credible solution to tackling one of the most significant causes of deal failure—seller's remorse." This counterintuitive approach will measurably turn the dial on the ratio of deals that reach successful conclusions.

—John Mill, attorney, MBO Coach

The Seller's Journey

How (Smart) Sellers Navigate the Obstacles to Selling Their Business

Denise Logan

Published and distributed by
Chase What Matters, LLC
Scottsdale, AZ
www.Chase-What-Matters.com
586-770-3329

ISBN: 978-1-7340447-0-6

Edited by Donna L. Dawson, CPE
Cover designed by Martin Gould
Page layout and proofreading by Sheila M. Mahoney

Printed and bound in Canada.

Contents

A Note to Readers

To the owners who have spent their lives building a business, the process of selling it is so much more than just a transaction. It is, in essence, the biggest transition of their lives.

When we choose to care for the emotions of the people involved in the sale of a business, it goes more smoothly, with fewer delays and less cost. It also helps owners land gently and gracefully on the other side of the sale, enriched not only with the financial rewards of what they spent their lives building, but with their spirits intact and their hearts ready to step into the next chapter of their lives.

Rather than make this a prescriptive "how-to" book, I invite you to come along on a journey with an owner who has sold his business. Given how treacherous the journey can be, and yet how awe-inspiring it can feel to safely make it to the other side, the tale is set in the wilderness of Glacier National Park. As an eavesdropper on our travelers, you will learn about the ways Marty and his advisors struggled to keep his deal on track, how they navigate slippery slopes of trust and how they consider a new path to rescue another traveler who has lost his way.

Although this story is loosely based on journeys I have taken with others, it is a composite of lessons I and my clients and their advisors have learned. The characters are a bit of me and a bit of you and a bit of anyone who has struggled with their identity and with navigating who they are, at work and in their lives.

I hope this story finds you at just the right time. If you are the owner of a business, I hope it encourages you to prepare for how you will exit your business. If you advise owners in the sale of their businesses, this book will help you understand and serve your clients in a way that will allow you to look back on your career and know that you have been involved in the sacred work of helping owners and their families navigate the perilous terrain of transferring their companies, their employees and their customers into safe hands. If you love someone who is struggling with the decision to sell their business or someone who serves them in this journey, the book will give you some understanding of the often overwhelming emotional process that sellers and their advisors are undergoing every day.

Lace up your boots and come along with us on *The Seller's Journey*.

Denise Logan

⋏ The Invitation

Normally Marty kept his cellphone off on weekends, but he couldn't resist peeking on this last Saturday in April. In fact, if he was honest, he was doing more than peeking this morning. He was pushing the refresh button obsessively on his email browser.

He just couldn't wait.

He didn't expect to feel the fluttering in his belly, even though his coach, Diane, had warned him he might.

The deliveries were happening right now. "Right now!" he thought. And even though he knew it wasn't likely that any of the recipients would call him the moment they received it, he wished he could be there, secretly seeing the looks on their faces when they opened the package.

Ding. It was a text from Diane. "How are you holding up?"

"The lizard is off the rails!" Marty replied.

Smiley face emoji followed by "Don't worry, they'll call" from Diane.

He knew it was a big deal for her to be texting, especially on a Saturday. She preferred the phone and, as she had taught him to do, she guarded her down time fiercely. He also knew she wouldn't call him now so he could keep the line free.

Refresh. Marty knew he was obsessing. Refresh. Refresh. He hadn't done this in months.

The cellphone in his hand rang. It felt like a relief, even though the caller was Marty himself, using the house phone to dial his cell just to make sure it was working. "Geez, I'm losing it," he thought.

His wife, Marjorie, couldn't help herself a second longer. She moved across the kitchen and slid his coffee mug out of the way, leaning in close, close enough for him to smell the floral scent of her soap. She wrapped her arms around his neck. "Marty, put the phone down and kiss me. You're about to give the gift of a lifetime and you'll pass out and miss it if you don't breathe."

Marty looked into Marjorie's green eyes as she stretched to kiss him. This time last year, he had wondered, "What the hell will I do with this woman when I retire? I don't even know her anymore." Their lives had drifted, what with raising kids and running the business. In fact, if it weren't for the grandchildren …

Ring! "Oh my God, someone's got it!"

Marjorie's hand flew to her mouth. Her raised eyebrows nudged Marty to answer it.

"Hello?"

"Are you freakin' crazy, Marty? I was cutting the grass when my wife said there was a delivery for me and the man insisted on handing the package to me himself. I thought I was getting served with a subpoena, or a pipe bomb or something from some crazy client."

Marjorie could hear the brash Jersey accent of Marty's attorney, Rob Court, booming through the phone. She hadn't imagined him as someone who cut his own grass, given the money she knew he earned.

"Well? Did you open it?" Marty asked

"You KNOW I did, you lunatic. Are you serious?"

Marjorie thought Marty looked just like their youngest son when he couldn't wait for her to open the gift he'd got her one Mother's Day years ago. She knew Marty was bursting to hear Rob's reaction.

"Yep. Dead serious, Rob. So, can you come?" Marty asked, trying not to give away how important it was to hear Rob say, "Yes."

"I'll be there. I mean, I've got to clear some things off my calendar but how could I say no to something like this?"

Beep beep. Another call was coming in. And then the house phone rang.

"Terrific, Rob! Listen, I've gotta go, that's Dan calling."

"Dan? Oh my God, Marty, you're bringing the whole team?"

"If they'll come!" And Marty was gone.

Across town, Rob hung up and said to his wife, "I never thought we'd see the day Marty would actually let go."

All afternoon, the conversations played out, one after the other, until Marty had heard some version of "Yes" from each of the people who had been instrumental in helping him sell his company. Rob Court, his attorney. Jim DeNovo, his banker. **8 people, 4 days, Glacier National Park**

Karen Walker, his accountant. Andrew McGill, his wealth manager. And Dan Perkins, the private equity investor who bought the business seven months ago. Of all of them, Dan was the one who Marty wondered whether he would *want* to invite on this trip when he first started talking about it.

And what a trip. With Diane and the guide, Liza, there would be eight of them, for four days in Glacier National Park, a place he had wanted to see more than anywhere else in the world since he was a kid.

Marjorie texted Diane as each of the calls came in. She knew Diane's pixie dust would be spinning as she celebrated Marty's connections with each of these people who had become surprisingly important to him.

As he finished the last call, from his accountant, Karen, Marty pushed the button to call Diane. How many times had he instinctively dialed her as soon as he finished a call, just to be able to say out loud what he was thinking so he could get a sense for what he was feeling? Somehow, he always felt better after they spoke. So it was comforting to hear her say this afternoon, "So, catch me up."

This time, though, Marty said, "I just wanted to say, the response has been amazing. But I think I need to catch up to myself first. Can we talk about it in detail on Monday? Marjorie and I are going for a paddle."

Diane's smile told her husband that all was right in Marty's world and they were now back to their own weekend, after just one more quick call.

"We've got all of them," Diane said when Liza answered her phone.

"That's great news!" Liza replied. Diane heard the rumble of thunder in the background and could tell Liza was on speaker phone. "Where are you?"

"I'm just getting the llamas into the barn before this storm rolls in. I had twelve teenagers out in the Smokies checking out the dogwoods today." That meant Liza was still in Gatlinburg, Tennessee, the home base for the tour company she ran.

A career change of her own had saved Liza's marriage and made the trips she had led with Diane and her clients over the years even more satisfying, especially when she saw how deeply connected guests became with nature and their own families as a result. Sometimes those trips came together quickly when one of Diane's clients needed a restorative boost so they could stick with a tumultuous business sale. Sometimes, like this trip with Marty and his team, they had months to plan something grander. There were still four months until they would journey into the backcountry of Glacier, and there was much to do. But none of it needed to be done right now.

"Get the girls into the barn, Liza. We'll talk next week," said Diane. "I just wanted you to know, we're on!"

"This is going to be the best one yet!" called Liza.

⋀ The Opposite of a Black Hole

The year before, Jim DeNovo, the investment banker helping Marty Tomlinson sell his business, had been thrilled to know that Marty had a plan for life after he sold. Except that it wasn't a real plan. Somehow, advisors hear a vague "travel and play golf" and delude themselves that it's enough of a vision to sustain a seller through the sale and beyond.

It was no surprise that when they got close to the finish line the first time, Marty started to get cold feet. The existential questions of "Who am I if I'm not the guy who owns this business?" and "What the hell am I going to do with myself all day?" had started to keep him awake at night.

But the kicker came when Marjorie told Marty one night, "Stop telling people you're going to buy a boat and sail around the world! There's no way in hell I'm going to live on a sailboat and be thousands of miles away from my grandkids!" He knew she didn't really like the water. In fact, he knew she was terrified of the water, but he'd always just sort of pictured her on the boat with him and figured she'd get over it and come along when the time came. "I mean, it was going to be a big-ass boat," he thought. How big is big? He was set to pull down $85 million from the sale; he wasn't buying a dinghy. But when Marjorie got serious and made her *no* loud and clear, Marty also knew he didn't really see himself going without her. Even when his buddies said they'd happily get the hell out of Dodge without their wives, he knew that wasn't what he'd do.

But the thought of abandoning his dream and doing—what? Sit around the house waiting for *Wheel of Fortune* to come on every night? That scared the shit out of him. He tried to figure out what he would do with himself. Golf would take him only so far. So, he did the only thing he could think of. He told Jim he'd changed his mind; he thought the price was too low.

Who am I if I'm not a business owner?

Jim was flabbergasted. They were eight weeks from closing at that point. "What the hell are you doing, Marty? You can't change the deal now! We've already gone this far. Just get some rest. The deal process can stress anyone out. You're gonna be fine." Marty was adamant: he needed more money—a lot more—or he was out.

The next day, Jim called Marty again. "Hey, Marty, how are you?"

Marty said, "Jim, I was serious yesterday. The buyers are screwing us over. I've been thinking about it and I'm not selling for a penny less than nine times EBITDA. They can take it or leave it."

"What?! Marty, listen, we've been over this a million times. A 6.2 multiple is great. The market is turning and you don't want to miss this window, man."

"Nope, no deal. My buddy told me I'm getting screwed on this. He knows of a company not in as good a market that got nine times and he said I'm a fool to let them take advantage of me. This is my life I've poured into this company, Jim, and if they don't want to pay what it's worth, fine. I'll just keep it and we'll find somebody else," Marty's voice was escalating.

"Somebody else? What are you talking about? You're not selling a house. We don't just stick a sign in the front yard and buyers come driving up with a sack of cash and make an offer! We've run a process here. You've already seen the earlier offers and they were much lower than Dan's. Plus, if you back out now, they'll sue you. We have a signed agreement."

"Fine. Let 'em sue. I'm not taking a penny less than nine times and that's final." Marty slammed down the phone and felt the rage in his head. "Bastards, thinking they can steal my company for a song!" He had almost convinced himself that the money really was the reason he was backing out, and not the terrifying thought that he was about to plunge into a black hole of despair and emptiness because he wasn't working.

Despite Jim's best efforts over the next ten days, he had been unable to persuade Marty to stay with it. In fact, Marty had stopped returning his calls or those of his attorney or accountant. He was sticking hard to his "my way or I'm out" line. They were burning time and Jim was having a hard time keeping Dan Perkins, the private equity buyer, in the deal.

"I think my seller's gone crazy," Jim said to Diane Richmond ten days after Marty had slammed down the phone. He told her what had happened.

"Yep, sounds like it," she said.

"Do you think you can get this deal back online?" Jim asked.

"Don't know, but let me have a conversation with him and we'll see. At the very least, if it looks like it's actually dead, everyone might as well pack up and go home instead of wasting more time and money." Diane checked her watch. She was one of the remaining dinosaurs who liked the feel of a watch on her wrist. "See if Marty is open to a conversation with me this afternoon or tomorrow morning. I'll make the time."

Diane knew that business owners feared the dreaded seller's remorse more than nearly anything else and it was what made them hold onto their businesses too long. That fear made them resist the efforts of well-meaning advisors to introduce them to the sale process.

Fewer than thirty percent of all businesses that went to market actually made it all the way through to a sale. Many abandoned the process along the way, often because the owner didn't have the emotional or financial stamina to make it all the way to the end, or because there was no one there to help them process the grief and loss and fear that arose when they first caught sight of what some sellers call "the abyss" that seemed to await them on the other side of a sale. Those who did speak of the unexpected and unfamiliar emotions they were facing were often told their feelings were petty or ridiculous or that they should suck it up and focus on what matters: the money.

Business owners who did reach the end of the sale process, Diane knew, had typically endured a grueling journey that may have lasted nine months or longer. That journey frequently left the seller with a sack of cash but feeling emotionally battered and bitter. That's what made them warn other business owners to avoid the wolves and hold onto their businesses at all cost, or at least until the dollar value they could get was big enough to outweigh the brutal emotional toll, a salve for the empty hole of their identity.

Marty's journey didn't have to end that way and Diane was determined to help him prepare to exit his business differently.

A few weeks after Diane had joined the team, when Marty was at his most frazzled, she asked him, "What would be a good celebration when we get to the other side of this closing?"

"Many shots of tequila on the beach and a month of sleep!" He was only half joking.

"No, seriously. What's one thing on your bucket list that you've given up hope of actually doing?"

What the hell am I supposed to do?

"Bucket list? Who has time to dream, Diane? It's all I can do to drag myself through the days to keep this company churning so those guys will want to close this deal and I can cash out."

"The cash again, Marty? Still trying to convince us both that the cash is really why you're doing this?"

"Sure, why else would I have ground myself down for the last 36 years, if it wasn't for the money?"

"C'mon, Marty, sing that song to somebody else. We've been in this together for long enough now for you to drop that facade with me. What's in there?" Diane tapped his chest, "right there, that you've wanted since you were a little boy but have given up on? Give it to me."

His shoulders slumped and he pinched the bridge of his nose to stop the tears from coming. Dammit, she always did that. Made him feel. "Nothing. I've got nothing I want. I just don't want to fall into the black hole of tedium that's waiting on the other side of the sale. Seriously, what the hell am I going to do with myself every day when I leave here?"

You *can* avoid seller's remorse

Money was never enough to get people through it when they got this scared.

"Hey, breathe, OK? Look at me," she said gently. She recognized that Marty's fear had just escalated and he was on the edge of shutting down because of the uncertainty. Together they sat quietly, breathing, helping his nervous system to calm so he could hear and process what they were talking about.

When his breath finally settled, Marty grinned. "You're right. It's not just about the cash. Although it *will* be nice to see it land in my account. Ka-ching! I just get freaked out about all the time that's going to be facing me when I'm finally outta here."

"That makes sense! But it's more than a year away, right? You'll still have a role here after the sale, remember? It's not like the morning after close you're out on your butt. Dan needs you to help transition the business into their portfolio so there's nothing jarring for your employees, your customers—or for you," she reminded him.

"I know, but eventually, I'm going to be out, done. Then what?"

"That's when you come back to The Plan. Remember The Plan? What you'll do the first week, the first month, the first quarter, the first year, the first three years?"

Marty and Marjorie had started with, "We'll travel and spend more time with the grandkids," when Diane first met them. Marty also had "golf, sleep and stop wearing a damned tie" on his list, even though Marjorie pointed out that he hadn't worn a tie in twenty years except to weddings and funerals, and even then she had to harangue him to put it on.

Diane and Marty had come a long way in a few short weeks. That's why she didn't believe his claim that he had nothing on his bucket list. She knew that was fear blocking his enthusiasm.

She asked him, "Do you still have your marble?"

"Seriously? I know Jim told you I was crazy when he first spoke to you about me, but are you actually worried I've lost my marbles?" Marty's humor was a good sign. His thinking brain was back online. She watched him fish into his pants pocket and pull out the big swirled marble. She had not been surprised when he had chosen the shooter. He's focused on showing me he's got balls, she had thought when he made the choice. She stifled a grin at the memory and thought how uncomfortable that had to be jangling around in his pocket with his keys every day. But if that's the reminder he needs to come back to what matters, who am I to make fun?

Diane slowed her breath and took Marty's hand, holding the marble.

"Marty, if this were the last marble in the jar, and you were making your peace, what would you say you're sorry you didn't get to do?" He knew the story of the jar.

He closed his eyes and really tried to feel it. He knew he couldn't give a glib answer; they'd done enough work that he knew Diane would have none of that, and he respected her too much to make a joke of it. Plus, he knew she was right. What *was* under there?

Even he was surprised when he heard himself say, "The glaciers. I've wanted to see them since I was little and I saw one in *National Geographic*." He couldn't resist saying that he'd happened upon the pictures of the glacier while he was actually looking for photos of a monkey.

"OK, so maybe we actually have two dreams to consider … a monkey and a glacier. Not sure they go in the same adventure, Marty, but who knows. It's your dream." Everyone had one.

Over the next weeks, as Marty continued to dream about glaciers and mountains, they were approaching their own summit: the deal was actually closing.

Diane had been preparing Marty and the deal team to make certain that his closing dinner would be special. Instead of the typical dinner focused on the bankers' and lawyers' success, she had shown them how they could celebrate in a way that acknowledged what *all* of them had done in service of the transaction while supporting Marty through the transition he was facing.

The focus of the evening was to stay on Marty, on allowing him to remain the center of attention, on hearing what he was feeling as he let go of the company that had been the focus of nearly four decades of his life. The professionals who had been shepherding Marty's deal had come to appreciate that while it was a transaction to them, to Marty it was a transition—the biggest one of his life.

On the night of the closing dinner, Marty had talked animatedly about his plans to see the glaciers and how everyone should come with him. There were polite murmurs of "that would be fun" and a few alcohol-fueled "absolutelys" from the assembled team. They all probably thought it was his pipe dream flowing into the generous rantings of a newly minted multi-millionaire. Diane might have been the only one in the room who noticed that Marty hadn't touched more than the first sip of the Dom from the initial champagne toast. She also knew that over the eighteen months that this deal had taken to get to closing, Marty had become attached to many of the people in the room. She wondered, "Is he serious?" and made a note to ask him about it in their next session.

Diane opted not to raise Marty's "glacial meltdown," as she had heard someone jokingly call it at the party, when they met for breakfast the next morning, mostly because Marjorie was joining them, as she sometimes did when their sessions were in-person. But she didn't have to: the perfume of the jasmine tea hadn't even begun to rise from the pot in front of Diane before Marty burst out, "So what do you think?"

"About what, Marty?" Diane wasn't taking the bait. He knew it from the way her left eyebrow raised that she was going to make him say it.

"About getting everyone from last night to go with me to see a glacier?"

Diane and Marjorie exchanged a glance, the kind you might exchange with your spouse as an excitable child asked whether you were going to the park yet five minutes after you had said, "We'll see." Except that Diane and Marjorie had different reasons for the look. Marjorie's said, "Can you believe this guy and his wacky ideas?" and Diane's said, "I hope Marty doesn't have plans to rope Marjorie into this adventure." Diane had gotten close to both of them over the past three months and had taught them to appreciate the other's perspective and to understand how both perspectives had helped them to raise their family and survive the precarious launching period twice: once when the kids went to college and again now, as they stood on the precipice of their new life.

Diane's "Mm-hm?" was noncommittal in an effort not to push either of them.

"It's gonna be great! We can get a team of Sherpas and …"

Diane noticed that while Marty was in full enthusiasm mode, Marjorie was using the breathing technique Diane had taught them. When Marty took a breath, Marjorie asked calmly, "Were you thinking of having the spouses go, too?"

Marty looked surprised at first and then he reached for her hand. "Oh babe, I wasn't, but only because I didn't think you would want to. Do you?" His hopeful enthusiasm was apparent.

Marjorie relaxed. "Thank God, Marty! I wasn't up for another explosion like the whole sailboat thing." She was quick to add, "But I wouldn't mind if you went, not at all. Please don't *not* go just because it's not my thing. I think you'll have an amazing adventure and I will enjoy watching you plan it."

"You're so wonderful," he said as he raised her hand to his lips. "And, this won't interfere at all with our trip to Greece, I'll make sure of it."

Diane thought, "They're really trying and it's absolutely a good sign for their future."

As the waitress came to take their breakfast order, Marty said, "I guess I'll have the steel cut oats this morning. No time like the present to start working on shedding this gut!" as he patted his belly.

"I guess he's serious," thought Diane, making a mental note to call Liza when she got back to her hotel.

⋀ A Better Bon Voyage

Marty and Marjorie spotted Diane as soon as she came into Union Station and started toward them. After a bit of chat about Diane's trip so far, the three settled into the waiting area.

Marjorie was trying not to fuss, but she was clearly nervous about the trip Marty and Diane were about to embark upon. Marty had been working with a trainer and dropped thirty-five pounds. He actually looked like a man in his fifties, instead of sixty-four. It had been good for him to have a goal to work toward this past year since selling the business.

During the first few weeks after the closing, Marty and Diane had noodled around what kind of trip he really wanted to take and what it would signify for him. In reality, it wasn't about summiting a giant mountain, it was about seeing a glacier, up close. Antarctica was on the table for a while, as was Greenland. They talked about an Alaskan cruise—that was probably something Marjorie would accompany him on. But Marty felt it was too tame. He wanted an adventure. And, he really wanted to take his team with him, the people who had helped shepherd him through the sale of his company. He didn't want to admit it at first, but he missed them. He had spent so much time with them over the eighteen months it had taken to sell the company. He had talked with his banker, Jim, and his lawyer, Rob, almost every day. He said to Diane, "I know it's ridiculous, but I feel lonely not talking to them. I mean, you can't just say to your lawyer, 'Can I just call you sometimes?'"

"Why not?"

"Because I'll sound like a nut or a needy little baby."

"But what if you don't say it like that? What if you're actually able to open up about what it has meant to have them walk this journey with you? The professionals in a transaction attach to their clients too, you know. It's just that no one ever talks about it. Let's look at a way to be able to tell them and get you what you need to feel connected to people who have served a really important role in your life."

He was glad to be more than just a deal to them

She knew that this very thing was part of what made launching hard for sellers. It's the same thing we see with our kids when they move from a favorite teacher at graduation or have to let go of their football coach. She tried to normalize emotions like that with her clients.

In the months after the closing, Marty had been able to keep in touch with Rob. They sometimes had lunch or played golf. And Jim's office was near his son's office downtown, so the three of them sometimes grabbed a drink in the evenings. Marty and Dan talked on the phone almost every day and saw each other when Dan was in town. That helped Marty feel less isolated and he found that he respected the work they had done for him even more because he didn't feel like he and his company had just been a commodity to them.

Since having the team come on this celebration journey with Marty was so important, he and Diane talked about doing something that wouldn't take all of them away from their families and work for too long so they would be more likely to come. He wanted something that was a challenge but didn't require them to become Olympic athletes. But it had to be something significant and befitting the moment. Finally, Marty decided on a trip to Glacier National Park in Montana.

Soon after Marty decided on the location, Diane reached out to Liza. Liza was the kind of guide who would take care of the logistics *and* care about creating an environment that would allow Diane to continue guiding the participants deeper into the emotional landscape that this trip would open.

Marty and Diane decided it was just going to be the principals, not their spouses and not any of his employees. That meant Marty plus four or five guests. With Liza and Diane, it meant planning a journey for eight travelers with different abilities and getting them aligned on the goals for the journey.

Marty initially wanted to do something grand—a two-week trip. Eventually, they settled on three nights. He joked that three nights sounded too much like the three-hour tour that landed the castaways on Gilligan's Island, so they added one more night at the end, just to break the curse.

They would have one night at Glacier Park Lodge, two nights at Granite Park Chalet and a final night at Lake McDonald Lodge. The trip would have them start on the east side of the 1,500 square mile national park in the Rocky Mountains, travel through the heart of the park and end on the western edge where it was easiest to reach the airport and disperse. It was an ambitious plan, and certainly it meant there were lots of parts of the park they wouldn't explore, but it set the scene for a grand adventure to the glaciers.

Because access to the park depended on the snow level each year, Liza suggested planning for September. Sometimes, if there'd been a particularly snowy winter, many of the trails still had snow pack until mid-August. By September, the trails would be clear and the families with kids would have headed home to start school, but the season was still temperate enough to enjoy day hikes and not freeze in the evenings. Marty chose the week after Labor Day for the adventure, which meant invitations needed to go out in April.

And by April, Marty and Dan had become so close that Marty couldn't imagine *not* including him in the trip.

In the months since the guests had each RSVP'd, there had been several video conferences in which the excitement had continued to build. In one, Liza outlined the trip in more detail, gave them some basic exercises to do so they would be physically prepared for the trip and provided a list of the things they would all need to take. Most of what they needed she would provide. That way, they each had to carry only a day pack, not full back-packing gear.

Marjorie was the first to spot Jesse in the train station. He had been a last-minute addition to the guest list when Marty's accountant, Karen, had to withdraw. Karen's father-in-law had gone into hospice the week before the trip and wasn't expected to last much longer. While her husband had urged her to go on the trip, saying he'd be alright, and she hated disappointing Marty and missing this once-in-a-lifetime journey with her long-time client, Karen knew that she would regret missing those precious moments with her family.

Karen's call to Marty had been filled with tenderness for both of them. Marty had missed being at his own father's bed-side. At that time in his life, work had been so all-consuming that he always thought he'd have another day to be with the people who mattered. Hearing Karen apologize for missing the trip, Marty was adamant that she not repeat his mistake. Her once-in-a-lifetime moment was with her family.

The old Marty would have been fuming that the money he had spent on securing a spot for Karen was wasted. But that hadn't even surfaced for him, a sign of how his former place at the center of the universe had been broadened to encompass the feelings and needs of people he cared about.

Marty asked Diane what he should do with the open spot. Should he just leave it open or should he invite one of his children (and how would he choose one without creating hard feelings)? Diane suggested he sleep on it and let the right answer emerge. She asked, "What is the trip actually about, Marty? And are you just trying to fill the spot with someone? Or are you marking a passage with people who were instrumental in getting you to this crossing?"

The answer came clearly the next morning when Marty and Dan were talking about an add-on acquisition they were hoping to close before the end of the year. The owner of that acquisition target was a stressed-out forty-something fellow named Jesse Tibia, who seemed to be having a hard time getting comfortable with letting go and with finding his place in the proposed larger company. Jesse had resisted any kind of coaching; he seemed stuck on needing to guard his ego and show Dan and Marty that he knew how to do everything.

He resisted coaching and guarded his ego

Right after ending a video call with Jesse, Marty texted Dan: "Got another quick minute?"

"Sure, what's up?" said Dan when Marty picked up his phone.

"I heard from Karen last night that she can't make the trip. Her father-in-law just went into hospice."

"Geez, that's rough for her. My wife's dad passed last year and hospice was terrific in the way they cared for him, but the uncertainty was crushing," Dan responded.

"Well, I was thinking that since we have an open spot on the trip, maybe we might ask Jesse to join us. What do you think? I mean, he's going to become part of the organization when we close on the acquisition. *If* we close it, that is. It might give him the comfort with us that he seems to be struggling with."

Dan said, "Interesting idea. But isn't this trip about you, Marty? It's supposed to be your time. I'd hate to feel like we're taking anything away from your celebration by adding Jesse and his stuff to the mix."

"I talked with Diane last night about filling the spot with one of my kids and she said to sleep on it and let the right answer show up," he said. "It just felt like a sign this morning when I saw how stressed out he was on our call. He's burning it at both ends and, in some ways, I feel like he's me from a year ago."

"Yeah, but do you think we could have convinced you to let down your guard enough to take several days away from the business and go hiking with us at this point in your deal?" asked Dan.

"Probably not, but then again you'd have never thought of it either because you were even more of a stressed-out mess than me! I heard Diane that afternoon when the two of you were in the lobby and she challenged you to go to your son's baseball game and leave your phone in the car."

"Well played, Marty, well played. You'd better try to reach Jesse today if he's going to get a flight on this short notice."

Marty was thrilled that Jesse was open to joining them on the trip. With about twenty years between them, Marty was hoping he'd get the chance with Jesse to mentor that he never had with his own sons, who had no interest in joining his business. Even with all the work he and Diane had done to prepare for his last day, his stomach still clenched when he thought of never again walking through the front door of the business home where he had spent so much of his life. Maybe he'd float the mentoring idea with Diane if they had private time on the trip. It would further ease his transition.

Diane had since spoken briefly with Jesse about what the trip was going to be like. She hadn't been involved in their deal with Jesse, other than a couple of conversations with Dan and Marty about what might be going on whenever Jesse seemed to shut down. But she liked the younger man and took it as a good sign that he was willing to join her and Marty in Chicago for the train trip to Glacier.

While Jesse hadn't originally thought he would want to give up the extra day to travel by train, when he'd seen the price of the airline ticket compared to the train fare, he told himself, "At least on the train I can catch up on the spreadsheets and probably make some calls." He had been worried about being away from the business for so many days. He'd told his CFO it was a due diligence trip, but honestly, he had read an article about the glaciers in *Outside Magazine* when he was burning time in a waiting room two weeks ago and had told himself it was something he'd like to see before he died. "Like that'll ever happen," his inner voice had said.

When Marty and Dan had called him the previous week, he had almost wondered if they were spying on him. Sometimes he wondered how those two guys seemed to get in his head and speak exactly to the issue that was bugging him in a way that helped put him at ease. Was it a sign that they were the right guys to get into bed with on this deal? He wasn't one to let his guard down easily and every time it happened with them, he found himself putting up walls again afterward. It was weird; he couldn't explain it. In the end, he decided that he'd know whether they were for real or not after spending some time with them. And, if it turned out they were assholes, at least he'd have gotten a free trip out of it. Marty had seemed oddly over the moon when Jesse had said yes and, while he wasn't used to trusting other men and was planning to be on his guard anyway, he admitted to himself that he wondered how the hell this guy had been able to let go enough to turn his baby over to a private equity firm. Much as Jesse wanted to feel that level of comfort, he couldn't imagine getting there and he knew time was ticking for him to fish or cut bait on this deal.

The train would give Marty, Diane and Jesse a day and a bit to settle in together and slow down before joining Liza and the others at the hotel across from the station in East Glacier Park Village.

"All aboard!" It was a flurry of goodbyes. Diane and Jesse walked ahead to the train to give Marjorie and Marty a private moment.

Once they were on board, Diane said, "Get settled in, you guys, and then we'll meet in the dining car for a drink. Thirty minutes, OK?" Diane disappeared through the sliding door into her own private berth and the train slipped through the tunnel out of Union Station.

⋀ Choose Your Traveling Companions Wisely

Marty was the first to arrive in the dining car and already had a gin and tonic in hand when Diane arrived. He popped two pretzels into his mouth and waved her over to the booth in the center of the car. They settled in easily together. Jesse joined them as the waiter was placing Diane's glass of Bordeaux in front of her.

"May I bring you a drink, sir?"

"Double Elijah Craig, single rock," said Jesse as he mentally debated whether to slip in beside Marty or Diane. He'd have preferred to be at a table; the booth felt awkward. He decided it was better to sit across from Marty than beside the older man. That way he could continue to size him up and it felt less weird to sit beside a woman in a booth.

Neither Jesse nor Marty had ever traveled any distance by train before, so the initial conversation was about their sleeping compartments and their impressions of the train so far.

"I love starting a trip with a car or train ride," offered Diane. "The hubbub of airports lately just stresses me out and I find the rhythm of the train allows me to ease gently into a vacation."

Jesse said he'd only been on the subway and commuter trains between New York and Boston, when he'd gone to MIT. He couldn't quite imagine what this trip would be like and admitted to himself that he was already feeling a little antsy knowing they had so much time ahead of them on the train. He wondered whether it had good wifi because he was hoping to get some work done and not have to sit here yakking with these two longer than was necessary to avoid looking like an unsociable jerk. Diane and Marty exchanged a glance as Jesse's phone buzzed again and he pulled it out of his pocket for the third time since joining them. They waited in silence as he returned the text.

"So, I know you're some kind of coach, but I have to say I don't really get what it is you do," Jesse said to Diane as his bourbon arrived. He took a big swallow.

"That's right, I am," said Diane. "I'm happy to tell you about what I do, but maybe you'd like to hear from Marty, to hear what it's been like from his perspective."

Marty jumped right in. "It's been like having a confidante, someone I could ask questions that I didn't think I could ask anyone else. In fact, and it was weird at first, but sometimes she knew the question I was struggling with even before I could put it into words for myself. Sometimes I was just pissed about something but couldn't even say what it was that had made me mad. We'd hop on the phone and I always felt better at the end of our call."

Jesse made a noncommittal noise. "Hmm; OK. I guess when I first …" he cut off in mid-sentence, his eyes drawn to the buzzing phone as he pulled it from his pocket again. He laid it on the table face up after texting a response.

"When you first …?" Diane asked.

Jesse stumbled on his words. "Um, I … don't remember what I was about to say there. So, how did you guys meet anyway?" He diverted the questions back to Diane and Marty. As Marty answered, happy to talk about their coaching relationship, Diane thought, "There's something going on there. It will be interesting to see what he's guarding and whether he finally feels enough at ease with us to let it out."

Marty was already mid-story when Diane tuned back in to what he was saying, "… it was stone cold dead and, really, I didn't know why the hell I should talk with this woman. But my banker,

Jim, told me it was on his dime and I didn't have to if I didn't want to. I'll admit, at first I was suspicious that she was just someone Jim had hired to talk me into changing my mind and I just wasn't going to. But I thought, 'What the hell; it's one call.'"

Diane was leaning back against the booth, tuning in to Jesse's energy as Marty popped another pretzel into his mouth. She noticed Jesse's eyes going to his phone on the table as a message popped up, but this time he didn't reach for it. She didn't know whether he was drawn into Marty's animated storytelling or whether he had decided the message wasn't worth answering; either way, she noted he had resisted the urge to disconnect from Marty.

She has a way of helping that's just ...

Marty continued, "I was pretty guarded in that first call. I sure as hell wasn't going to be talked into taking a penny less than my company was worth and I made her work pretty hard to get more than just a 'yup' or an 'uh-huh' out of me."

Diane smiled, remembering how Marty had had his tough-guy "just try to change my mind, lady, and I'll shut you down" attitude going on that call.

Marty said, "When I realized she really was interested in understanding me and wasn't just a lackey trying to get me to do what my banker or the buyer wanted me to do, I started to open up and Jesse, I'll be damned, but that woman," he nodded toward Diane, "has a way of helping that's just ... hard to explain. Before I knew it, I was caught up in this crazy conversation about lizards ..." Jesse made a "what the hell?" face at "lizards" and Diane noticed he had leaned back against the back of the booth, skepticism flooding his face, "... and I saw things I'd never even thought were going on under the surface with other people. And myself."

Marty noticed that Jesse had withdrawn—something he wouldn't likely have picked up on a year ago—and he caught himself. He had become so enthusiastic talking about what had changed for him that his voice has grown loud and he knew he was overwhelming Jesse. He paused and took a swig of his gin and tonic and leaned back. "I could go on and on about how this changed everything for me, the way it helped me to see what was keeping me from doing what I needed to for my business. But also how it helped change even the way I interact with my wife."

It took some time for trust to build

"And it took some time, didn't it, Marty?" Diane prompted, a little uncomfortable that Jesse might think they were trying to sell him on coaching. "It took some time for trust to build between us and for you to see that it wasn't some weird New Age thing, and then open up and ask for help."

Turning to Jesse, she said, "It's not right for everyone, this kind of coaching, and I want to assure you I have no intention of psychoanalyzing you this week. We're all just out together to relax and celebrate with Marty on this trip he's been dreaming of for so long. It's really wonderful that you are along with us, Jesse." She touched his right arm gently. He flinched ever so slightly and she apologized. "Sorry, I'm a hugger and forget that we've just met."

Jesse's face flushed. "I'm just a little on edge, is all. I haven't been sleeping lately." He motioned the waiter to bring another round of drinks, even though Diane shook her head and covered her still half full wine glass with her hand.

Marty took the last swig of his own drink as the waiter set down the fresh ones for him and Jesse and said, "Marjorie used to make me drive the kids around the block for hours to get them to fall asleep when they were little. Maybe you'll get the same bonus from the rocking of the train tonight, buddy."

The conversation shifted away from business to talk of kids and then to vacation memories from the three travelers' childhoods; soon it was time for dinner. Jesse noticed when he took the menu from the waiter that the sky was starting to show the first colors of what promised to be a bold sunset. How long had it been since he'd noticed the sunset, he wondered. His wife used to set the timer on her phone for twenty minutes before sunset every night when they were first married. She would fly up out of her chair when it sounded and pull him to the front door, insisting they see every sunset together. At first he thought it was silly, but it made her so happy to walk to the end of their road and wait for the orange ball to drop, her wrapped in his arms, his chin resting on her blond hair, the fruity scent of her shampoo filling his nose, and neither caring that the dishes would be waiting for them when they got home. Jesse was shaking his head, lips pursed together, when Marty asked, "No what, man?"

"Huh?"

"You were shaking your head no, so I wondered what you were saying no to."

"Nothing. I was just thinking about how my wife and I used to make a point of watching the sunset every night and I can't even remember the last time I noticed the sunset. You know; kids, work, stuff. Sometimes it all feels like so much. But seeing it now made me realize how much she would love going on a train trip like this. White tablecloths, the little drapes on the windows, the sunset over the fields. Wait, what kind of crop is growing there?" asked Jesse, pointing out the window.

Then Marty and Jesse were debating whether they would see more corn, wheat or soybeans along the way. "Corn," said Diane, as she nudged Jesse to let her out of the booth to use the ladies' room after the waiter had taken their orders. "City boys!" she tossed over her shoulder with a satisfied grin as she walked away.

When Diane returned to the table, Jesse and Marty were talking sports. After she slipped back into the booth and Jesse settled in beside her, she simply enjoyed watching the landscape slide past in the picture window, missing her own family and wishing she was enjoying this trip with them, too. Like Jesse's wife, she loved the transitions between night and day—both sunrise and sunset—and tried to see as many of them as she could.

Conversation over the meal moved easily from topic to topic and although the two men frequently lapsed into shop talk, much of which was beyond Diane's knowledge, she enjoyed watching them talk over subjects that clearly interested them. She guessed that the third round of drinks had also loosened

Jesse's grip on his guard and she wondered to what degree alcohol had become a coping mechanism for this man who was so driven to make a success of himself.

By the time dinner was over, the sun had fully disappeared into the unique darkness of the Great Plains. No moon, but the first few stars were showing in the darkened sky. Occasionally, they would spot a farmhouse with windows lit, the people inside likely unaware that strangers were whooshing past, glimpsing, now and then, their little family moments.

Although the waiter offered dessert, two of the three declined sweets, conscious of the work they had put into their fitness regimens over the past several months in preparation for the trip. Jesse asked for an espresso and when the waiter apologetically told him the machine was out of order, he turned to Marty and said, "How about a nightcap, then?" It was then that Diane excused herself to return to her sleeping berth. "I'm hoping for some of that rock-a-bye-baby sleep Marty mentioned earlier. I wish you the same."

⋀ Fear Is Just Excitement Without Oxygen

Diane was enjoying a bright floral tea, sitting with her journal in the dining car when Jesse's voice startled her as he approached from behind. It was already past noon. Apparently sleep had found him.

"I have to say, I'd have never guessed that Marty could drink like a college boy!" he said, popping two Advils while appropriating the last of Diane's orange juice. His sheepish grin as soon as his lips were on the glass told Diane he had just realized his mistake.

"No problem," she told him, trying not to laugh out loud. "We're all going to be in close quarters over the next few days; might as well start behaving like siblings, right? What's mine is yours?"

"My wife hates that I still drink milk straight out of the carton, and tells me it's barbaric, but it just doesn't taste the same out of a glass."

"I'll remember that and make sure I pour milk on my cereal in the morning before you get up," she teased him.

"Hey, Marty tried to explain to me what the lizard thing is last night. But I'm not sure the fourth drink made it likely that he would be able to explain it or I'd be able to understand it. But it sounds cool and I wouldn't mind hearing about it. That is, if it's not a secret."

"Sure." Holding up her left hand she said, "Your hand is like a visual representation of your brain." Pointing to her thumb, "The thumb is the amygdala. Ah-MIG-da-la," she sounded out for him. "It's the oldest part of our brain, the fear sensor—the 'reptilian' brain, if you like. Its job is to constantly scan the environment for danger, so it serves a useful purpose—it helps ensure our survival." She moved her thumb back and forth like a watchful creature. "Say, for example, that you were attacked by a black bear when you were a boy. As an adult, the amygdala would spot a big black dog and think *bear!* It would signal you to run. The problem is that it can't distinguish between what *is* and *isn't* genuine danger. It relies mostly on pattern recognition. Now play along," she said, motioning for Jesse to hold his hand up like hers. "Tuck your thumb across your palm like this, and wrap your fingers over the top, like this."

"Oh, buddy, she's got you making the little girly fist!" Marty bumped into Diane's chair from behind as the train was slowing for a stop. "I'll fight you anytime if you're dopey enough to put your thumb inside your fist."

Diane rolled her eyes at Marty, "Never mind him, Jesse, keep your thumb inside your fist. You can clock him with a proper manly fist later if you like!" Jesse put up his dukes.

"C'mon, Marty, let Jesse pay attention while you find the waiter to refill my tea and get you guys some strong coffee—sounds like you need it, from what I heard went on after I went to bed."

Both men feigned ignorance and looked at each other as if to say, "Whatever could she mean?" They were becoming playful co-conspirators and Marty was grinning as he moved further into the dining car in search of the waiter.

"So, back to your brain," Diane continued. "With your thumb tucked inside and your fingers wrapped over the top, we have a good representation of your brain. Remember, the amygdala, the fear sensor, is tucked securely inside. The fingers wrapped over it represent your prefrontal cortex." She was using the index finger of her right hand to point to the parts of her left-hand brain model. "The prefrontal cortex is the thinking part of the brain. It's where logic comes into play and it helps us to make decisions. Now, move your thumb around inside that fist. What do you notice?"

"It doesn't move very much," answered Jesse.

"So, move it around more assertively. What do you notice now?"

"The fingers aren't quite so snug anymore on top and it takes more force to keep them down, to keep the thumb still," he answered.

"Exactly. Remember that the thumb is the fear sensor and the fingers wrapped around it are the thinking brain. So, watch this," she said. "If the thumb, the amygdala, gets activated enough, it will pop the fingers all the way up." She demonstrated as she said, "You'll literally flip your lid!"

The amygdala can't distinguish genuine danger

She could almost see the lightbulb go on above Jesse's head as he realized what she had just shown him, and he was mirroring it with his own hand. As he flipped his own "lid," he smiled in surprise at what he had just seen. "Wow! I never thought of that!" he said.

"So, we call the amygdala the lizard as shorthand to express the idea that fear might be running the show. Marty, actually, takes great joy now in being able to say that his lizard is showing."

"Talking about my big ol' lizard, are you, now?" said the older man as he rejoined Jesse and Diane at the table. Diane shook her head and rolled her eyes as she always did when he said it, but especially because the waiter was walking up right behind him with menus and was unable to conceal his surprise at what he had just heard Marty say. They both knew, though, that this visual tool had helped Marty understand what was going on inside and had lessened his previously inexplicable reactions—they had looked like anger, but were really fear.

After the waiter had taken their lunch orders, Marty excitedly prompted Diane, "Tell him the rest!"

"There's more?" said Jesse, looking from Marty to Diane.

"Yep. Since we have your handy-dandy hand to use as a prop, open your hand like this," she said, holding her hand upright, palm facing forward. "So, fear generally shows up in one of five ways." She ticked them off slowly, one finger at a time: "Fight, flight, freeze, fawn or submit." Diane noticed the fleeting look on Jesse's face that said "I know this already" when she began, but she also saw that by the time she finished, he had realized he was learning something and his interest was re-engaged.

Fight, flight, freeze, fawn or submit

"Say those again?" he said.

"Fight, flight, freeze, fawn or submit," she repeated. "You've probably heard of fight and flight, right? And maybe freeze?"

Jesse nodded. "That's the deer in the headlights look, right?"

"Exactly," said Marty. Diane liked that Marty was so engaged in seeing Jesse learn something.

"But you probably don't know these last two … fawn and submit. Fawn is like brown-nosing or people-pleasing and it sounds like this: 'Yep, yep, I'll get you those documents, right away, right away!'" Diane was speaking quickly and nodding her head vigorously. "It's basically the amygdala saying, 'I'll do whatever you want, just don't hurt me!' And submit sounds like this: 'Fine, have it your way! I'll do what you want.'" Diane said with a mock resigned frown as she shrugged her shoulders and threw up her hands.

"Oh my God, I've seen all of these!" said Jesse.

"Yep," said Marty. "Just wait till you hear the next part."

"Do you want to tell it?" asked Diane.

"Sorry, no, it's your show," he said, in a lower tone and with a slightly sheepish face.

"Hey, I'm not chastising you Marty," Diane said. "I really mean it. You've lived this over the past year. You're welcome to chime in."

Marty turned to Jesse and said, "Did you see it? That, just now, was the lizard, scared I was in trouble, it made me pull back."

"Seriously?" said Jesse, looking to Diane, who nodded.

"Wait, let me understand this," he said, waggling his thumb. "This is the … lizard, the …"

"Amygdala," chimed in Marty.

"And this is the thinking brain," Jesse said as he folded his fingers over his thumb, making what Marty called the girly fist.

"Yep, keep going," encouraged Marty.

"And if the lizard gets scared enough, it flips my lid," he said, making the motions with his hand.

"Exactly."

"But you didn't look flipped out—did I miss something?" Jesse asked.

Diane walked Jesse through the realization that all day long each of us is walking around in various states, from "safely tucked in," with our thinking brain fully engaged, all the way up to being fully wigged out. She demonstrated with her two fists, opening and closing each again and again. "It depends on what your amygdala has spotted and how unsettled you are moment to moment."

"That's crazy!" said Jesse. "How do I stop that from happening?"

"You don't," said Diane. "But you can recognize when it's happening and practice ways to calm the reactivity in yourself and learn to recognize it in others."

Jesse was fully engaged in the conversation now and actually looked startled when their meals arrived.

"I could keep going," Diane said. He nodded as he took a big gulp of coffee and reached for the ketchup for his fries.

> You can recognize it and calm the reactivity

"So, all of us will use all of these fear responses—fight, flight, freeze, fawn and submit—at different times to react to what has frightened us. But we each typically have two or three favorites that naturally show up. Mine go like this: first I freeze, then I fawn and, if that doesn't work, you can almost watch me run straight into flight. Make no mistake, though; if those don't work, I may end up in fight or submit, but they're not my go-to responses."

She nodded her chin to Jesse, before taking a sip of her now-cool tea. "What do you think yours are?"

"Hmm … I don't know." He cocked his head to the right and looked up to the left, thinking.

Marty couldn't wait; he was dying to tell his, and Diane was almost surprised that he wasn't raising his hand in the air like an anxious second-grader who knew the answer. Finally, "I can tell mine!" he volunteered, and he looked a bit ashamed and worried that he had overstepped again.

"Go ahead, Marty," Diane prompted, "it'll help Jesse to hear yours."

"So," he said, pointing to the ring finger of his outstretched hand, "I start with fawn. Then, when I get frustrated, I drop to submit," wiggling the pinkie. "But, God help us, when the resentment that creates builds up, I jump into FIGHT!" He poked his index finger right into Jesse's chest. The younger man bristled and then realized Marty had intentionally provoked him.

"Ah, you almost got me there, old guy!" said Jesse as his shoulders dropped and the smile spread across his face. "Watch it, though, I could easily drop you!" The two threw fake punches at each other from their chairs.

"I'd rather see you arm wrestle, but we'll save that for the quiet nights when we're in the woods, with nothing else to do," joked Diane. "That will help me figure out which of you I'll call on to defend me from any rogue grizzly bears we come upon on the trail. So what did you discover right then, Jesse?" bringing the conversation back to the topic at hand, so to speak.

"I guess … I fight as my first response when I feel threatened," he answered.

"And, what comes next if fight doesn't work?" she asked.

"Hmm, then I guess I just walk out. Which one is that?"

"Flight," she answered. "Does that seem right?"

"I guess so."

"Tell us about a time when you've been in an argument and how it ended," she prompted.

"I dunno if I should say … I don't think I should tell tales. But when my wife just keeps pushing me about something, I get loud, and then if she keeps it up, I'll just grab my helmet and take off on my motorcycle until I've cooled down."

"And, how does that usually work out?" Diane asked with a little smile.

"Not so great. Usually, by the time I calm down and come back, she'll have left me twenty voicemails or texts."

"What do they usually say?"

"The first ones are usually a mix of mad and sad, but as she keeps on texting or calling, they seem more like she's pleading, almost begging me to call her or come home." Jesse said. "It's pathetic."

"And how does that make you feel?" she asked.

Briefly, Jesse was taken aback by the question—his head jerked back ever so slightly and his eyebrows dropped. "I dunno," he said curtly. Then Diane saw him relax slightly. She said nothing, giving him space to continue or not. "I guess I feel a mix of regret for storming out, but sometimes I also just ride further, not wanting to go home because I feel guilty and she seems so needy. But, you know, the make-up part is usually pretty good." He grinned at Marty.

Diane moved her arms so the waiter could take her empty plate. She said to Jesse, "Nice opener for me. You'd be a great straight man if I ever take my act on the road, Jesse. Want to know why that happens?" she asked him.

"Sure! It'd be great to not keep going over the same shit day in and day out with her."

Diane lined up three props to illustrate the example she was going to use. She set the pepper shaker on the left, the little bin of sweeteners in the center and the salt shaker on the right. Marty leaned forward with his coffee cup between his palms. Although he'd seen this several times, he liked the clarity of it. Besides, he and Marjorie sometimes still played out the drama

Jesse had described, just without the motorcycle, so a refresher wasn't a bad thing.

"Jesse," Diane explained, "you know that as humans we're wired to attach to other people, right?" He nodded. "As babies, if we don't attach, we die. It's plain and simple, and you likely watched it with your own kids when they were babies." He nodded again, tilting his head, trying to lock in what she was saying.

"Because attachment is so critical to our survival, the amygdala senses any type of disruption in our attachment—either too much or too little—as danger. Remember, the lizard is always watching for danger, but isn't that smart." Jesse nodded.

"There is a metaphor that a psychobiologist named Stan Tatkin created to help us visualize how each of us attaches differently. We typically learn it as infants or young children, and it's a coping mechanism to help us manage the fear the amygdala senses about attachment." She continued, lifting the pepper shaker on the left. "This is an Island." She put it back down. Lifting the sweetener bin in the middle, she said, "This represents an Anchor." Finally, she lifted the salt shaker on the right. "This represents a Wave. The Island, Anchor and Wave are on a continuum of how we deal with attachment.

Humans are wired to attach to each other

"An Anchor," she said, lifting the sweetener bin, "can withstand a certain amount of rockiness in any relationship without pulling away or getting scared that the other person is leaving." She put it down and picked up the pepper shaker on the left. "But the Island, when it seems that things are rocky or that someone is overwhelming, will do this," she pulled the pepper shaker far to the left. "It's why it's called an Island: in the face of emotional distress or upset, the Island pulls away, isolates."

"Oh, I get it, like running off to a deserted island," said Jesse.

"Exactly. Now, get this." She lifted the salt shaker on the right end of the continuum. "When there is a disagreement or this kind of person thinks the other person is pulling away, the

Wave rushes in. Often we'll hear things like, 'Are we OK?' over and over, or we see the need to get closer."

"Oh my God, that's my wife and me! I'm an Island, I pull away. And she's like a damned tsunami flooding over me." He paused. "Sorry, that was mean, to say that about her. I mean, we're good."

"And what happens?" Diane asked.

Marty jumped in, swooping up the salt and pepper shakers, showing how the more the Island moves away, the faster the Wave chases it and the farther the Island then pulls away, creating a loop of increasing distress for both.

"So when I grab my keys and jump on my bike, I'm reacting like an Island?"

"Yep. Typically, you've done it because in the argument, you've reached the point where your amygdala is so triggered you've flipped your lid, and the fight has switched to flight and you run." He was scratching his unshaven chin. Diane continued, "The drag of it is that because the argument has also flipped *her* lid, she keeps after you, trying to get you to attach. Remember—the amygdala perceives danger, even more so as you start detaching. It makes her start to push you for connection, and as you pull away, her Wave becomes a tsunami of fear. When you leave, and she can't reach you and doesn't know if or when you'll return, the calls she's making are because her amygdala is reading that as a dangerous disruption in her attachment with you. We attach or we die as babies, but the lizard can't tell the difference when we're adults."

"How do I fix it?" Jesse asked.

"There are several things you can do. First, be aware that you're wired to fight and then flee. When those signals of upset from the lizard start to rise, you can pause, notice that you're afraid—remember, this is all fear driven—and calm down, so the automatic response doesn't take over and you can figure out with your thinking brain what to do next. But, if you get to the point where you've flipped your lid, and you're about to bolt for the door and jump on your motorcycle—which I highly discourage since your thinking brain is offline—you can say to your wife, 'I'm upset and I'm going to take a break. But I *will* be back. And we can try to find a way to talk about this when we're both more settled.' That will help her to not go full Wave.

"And if she does anyway, you can recognize that the more Island you go, the more you trip her fear and the more Wave she is likely to become. Sometimes, just being aware that what she's doing is because she's afraid can help to break the spell of fight or flight that's going on in you."

"Man, that's a lot!" said Jesse, rubbing his face.

"It is!" Marty agreed. "And, I learned that it's not just going on between Marjorie and me. This same thing is playing out between me and my employees, between me and my customers and with vendors. In fact, until Diane helped us get a grip on it, it was exactly what was killing the deal between me and Dan."

Jesse looked perplexed, and leaned in with interest. "How so?"

Diane nodded to Marty to continue. "Well, remember how I told you I almost blew up my deal because Marjorie said she wouldn't go on the sailboat trip with me?"

"Yeah."

"Well, I didn't know it then, but it was my fear that made me come up with a demand for some crazy number I knew they couldn't produce so I could get out of the deal and still save face.

Slowing down to deal with emotions ...

I mean, I didn't want to say I was pulling out because my wife wouldn't let me do what I wanted to when I retired! That would make me look like a wimp."

Jesse nodded and pursed his lips, considering what Marty had just shared. "Makes sense."

Diane added, "And, when Marty did that, the banker and the buyer both got scared and their amygdalas started running *their* reactions."

"Yep, the more times Jim and Dan called me, the more I backed up. Which I had no idea at the time was making them *more*, not less, likely to keep hounding me." Marty picked up the salt and pepper shakers. "We were caught in a crazy Island-Wave chase all over the place." He demonstrated, then put the shakers back down, one on either side of the sweetener bin. "That is, until Diane got involved and helped us all calm the hell down." He showed with his fist how the fingers settled back over the thumb, showing the thinking brain coming back online and protecting the frightened amygdala.

... **leads to fewer delays and less cost**

"So *that's* what you do as Marty's coach, huh?" Jesse asked Diane.

"More or less. I've been called 'The Seller Whisperer,' although in fairness, I'm actually helping all the parties to manage their normal and to-be-expected emotional distress in what is typically the single biggest transition of their life."

"Transition, you called it? It's just a sale." said Jesse.

"I did. And sadly, too many people treat sellers like it's just a transaction, ignoring the human emotions involved in what is, in essence, a huge life transition," she said, intentionally pausing to sip her tea before continuing. "When we are able to slow things down enough to care for the emotional side of what's going on for the people involved in the transaction, it actually goes smoother, with fewer delays and less cost. And, instead of leaving an emotionally wrecked seller filled with remorse, we're able to use the transition to help them land gently and gracefully on the other side of the sale, ready to step into their new life."

"*That's* what this trip is about, buddy-boy!" said Marty, clapping Jesse on the shoulder, just as the conductor came on the loudspeaker to announce that they would be arriving at East Glacier Park Village, Montana, in 45 minutes.

"Wait? We're here already? This trip has blown by. I never even got to the spreadsheets I was going to work on," said Jesse. "But this stuff has been fascinating. Really."

Diane smiled as she noticed the waiter was approaching with the check. Marty followed her glance and said, "I'll take care of this. And then I've got a few things to do in my cabin before we arrive. See you guys on the platform?"

"Thanks, Marty, that's very gracious of you to pick up the check. I appreciate you," said Diane.

"Yeah, man; thanks," Jesse said.

Diane added, "Liza will be waiting for us at the hotel. I can hardly wait for you to meet her!"

The three went to gather their belongings from their berths, each thinking about the conversation that had filled their afternoon.

⋀ Friends Make for a Better Journey

Excited passengers filtered off the train and gathered their luggage. Jesse was surprised that the big brass-rimmed thermometer on the train platform read seventy-two degrees.

"Don't get used to it," said Marty, following Jesse's gaze. "I've been watching the temperatures for the week ahead and it's gonna be pretty nippy at night, especially close to the glacier." His excitement was bubbling up. He was going to see a glacier tomorrow!

Marty recognized Liza from their video calls during the planning stages, but he was unprepared for how strongly she embraced him once she'd let go of Diane. "Oh Marty, this is going to be *such* a memorable trip!" she said. Marty hadn't really been a hugger, but this past year, he had become comfortable with lots of things that hadn't been part of his gruff, buttoned-up professional life. "I actually think I'm going to have fun," he thought, and was surprised that some part of him had thought he might not.

"You must be Jesse," Liza said, extending her hand. She had noticed the subtle way he took half a step back as she approached and decided not to give him her bear-hug welcome.

After the short walk to the hotel, Marty stepped into the historic Glacier Park Lodge. He was amazed at the Douglas fir logs towering over the lobby. "I've been looking at the website and

Marjorie told me she thought I'd wear the print off the brochure you sent me, but Liza, this is even better than I imagined!"

Liza beamed. She enjoyed bringing people's dreams to life and was in no rush to push the group through the spectacular lobby of the 1912 hotel. She had noticed that Marty had talked almost non-stop from the train platform and that he had struggled a bit to keep up with Jesse's hurried pace. It took effort to suppress her frown as Jesse pulled his phone out of his pocket and his face dropped into the familiar slack expression once the screen pulled his focus away from what surrounded them. She wondered whether either of them had been able to take in any of the scenery on the train trip or as they walked the 300 yards to the hotel from the train.

She knew, from years of doing these trips with Diane, that her friend had probably kept her traveling companions alternating between periods of introspection, conversation and attempts to get them to enjoy watching the countryside pass outside the train's windows. But Liza loved drawing her guests into the tiny moments that were the backbone of every adventure she planned.

"Hey, did you guys notice Dancing Lady Mountain?" She motioned to the bellman to take their bags, telling him which rooms were for each. "I've already checked you in, and David will take your bags to your rooms. Let's just get a little walk in and then I'll send you off to settle in before dinner."

Jesse slipped the phone back into his pocket. Liza got them outside and fully immersed in the majesty that surrounded them, pointing out the peaks and orienting them in their new surroundings. Her friend would continue to ground them in what was real, although neither woman thought it would last once they sent their guests to their rooms and they had access to wifi again.

"Awe-mazing!" Marty said as they returned to the lobby.

Even though Diane rolled her eyes at his pun, saying "You've been working on that, haven't you, Mr. Smarty Pants?" she was thrilled to see the bright smile and brighter eyes twinkling back at her.

"Yep, and don't get tired of it. I'm pretty sure there's going to be even more 'awe'-ful ones to come," he said as the others groaned.

"Take a little walk if you like, Marty, or just enjoy the awe-mazing view some more. We'll meet in the lobby at 5:30 for dinner. OK?" Liza hugged him again. Marty was surprised that he was already hugging her back, although conscious that this tiny woman was stronger than he first thought.

The deal totally changed their view of the sales process

Liza handed Jesse his room key. "It's your last name and room number," answering his question about the wifi password before he could even get it out.

"That obvious, huh?" he said with a half-smile that said "busted."

"Yep, I could tell you were antsy with the last part of our nature tour. Don't worry, it takes time to settle into a slower rhythm, even after the train trip. I see it all the time," she shrugged.

Diane winked and said, "Same time we told Marty, OK?"

Half an hour later, Marty shouted to two men halfway across the lobby. "Can you believe it? We're really here!" His long-time attorney, Rob Court, and Jim DeNovo, the banker who had helped him sell the company, had known each other casually for years, but this transaction with Marty had changed the way they saw the process and they had already closed two other deals since his, more smoothly than they had ever imagined.

"Hey, buddy, it's great to see you!" Rob socked Marty in the shoulder as Marty pulled him in for a hug. Rob really was excited to spend this time with Marty. His client looked happier than he'd seen him in all the years he'd known him. It had been no small feat to get his own knees ready for this trip. He hoped he wouldn't be the laggard on the trail; that would be embarrassing, especially since he and Marty were close to the same age, and it was clear that Marty had been taking his training seriously. "I wonder if my wife's been talking to Marjorie—she's been bugging me about what's on my bucket list lately."

"You're lucky she didn't hand you a mop to go with that bucket, Rob. I hear you've been cleaning up your act," joked Jim. He took Marty's bear hug in stride, even though Jim was fully two heads taller than him and it felt weird to have Marty's head against his chest in the embrace. Jim knew that Marty had been feeling really emotional as he approached the end of his earn-out period with the company. In the past, he'd never even thought about what his clients might have been feeling, especially not a year after he closed the deal. It had been different to continue having contact with a client, and it was certainly unheard of, before Marty, to do anything like this trip to celebrate a deal. Usually the closing dinner was a kind of drunken hoedown after which everyone was off to the next big deal. But this woman Diane had changed a lot of how he thought about his clients and the way he did his deals.

They had never considered how their clients were feeling

Their laughter drew Diane and Jesse from the chairs where they'd been sitting with Marty before Jim and Rob arrived. Rob and Jim warmly greeted Diane as she and Jesse joined the group. They were working on other things together, but it was always a delight to get to spend time with the people she worked with in a more casual setting.

"This is Jesse Tibia. He's thinking of joining Dan and me and bringing his company under the big tent," said Marty.

"Hey Jesse, good to meet you," said Rob, shaking hands. Jesse thought, thank God these people are not going to hug me. He'd been reluctant to join them, especially once he saw Marty hugging them. Diane had been the one to say, "C'mon" and he'd tagged along with her to meet the others, but tried to stay an arm's length back.

"Dan-o!" said Jim as Dan Perkins joined the group. The plaid-shirted, red-haired man who joined them was one of the faces familiar to most of the group. Dan wasn't the kind of guy you would peg in any group as the one with the money, but his private equity firm had put money into some of the most successful companies in the world and his ability to spot a good one and build something great alongside a founder was legendary. As a banker, Jim loved doing deals with Dan. He was the kind of unassuming, stand-up guy Jim trusted. And Jim didn't trust many people in his business. He surprised himself by giving Dan a back-slapping hug when he walked up. "Hey, what's Marty doing to you, Jim? You're a hugger now, too?" said Dan.

"Glad you're here, Jesse," said Dan, nodding in the direction of the man he could tell was uncomfortable with all this physical contact. "It's gonna be good," he reassured him. Jesse felt himself relax and then caught himself; his guard went back up.

Liza walked up to them with Andrew McGill, Marty's wealth advisor. "This is awesome, Marty! Liza was just showing me the historic Red Bus," Andrew said. "Can you believe those vintage babies from the Thirties still run?" He clapped Marty on the back and shook hands with the others. "You must be Jesse," he said. "Good to know ya." He shook Jesse's hand before he wrapped Diane in a hug.

"OK, everybody hungry?" asked Liza. "The van's out front and I've planned something special for tonight, so let's get going."

Over dinner at the Izaak Walton Inn, where they dined in a historic railway car, Liza outlined what the next couple of days would look like. Wrapping up, she said, "After dessert, we'll head back to the lodge. You're welcome to hang out in the lounge, but I suggest you resist the temptation to make it a late night. We'll get a very early start tomorrow, because we're going to drive to the trail head just beyond Logan Pass."

"How far is that?" asked Dan.

"About sixty miles. While that might not sound like far, on the mountain roads it can be slow going and sometimes fog or wildlife or rock slides can add significantly to the travel time. We hope to be able to step onto the trail by 7:00 AM. That means we leave the lodge by 4:45." Several of them groaned. "I've made arrangements for the lodge to pack travel breakfasts for us so you can eat in the van. And yes, they will have coffee for those who need it. I've got a couple of big travel thermoses so you can get refills along the way, plus water for everyone. Remember to stay hydrated. We are at elevation and will be climbing and no one is happy with a nasty dehydration headache. So maintain a two-to-one water to coffee ratio. I have lots of water, so no need to ration it. And I've got snacks to keep your energy up, too." Liza checked her notes before continuing.

"So please be in the lobby at 4:30 AM, fully packed and ready to go. You'll leave your luggage in the van and just take your day packs with you for the hike. You got a list of the things to put in your day pack and if you need a refresher, circle up with me when we get back to the lodge. I've arranged for the bulk of our supplies to be waiting for us at the chalet so we don't have to pack it all in. I didn't want you to have to lug sleeping bags, ice crampons, poles and food. It's enough to just make the trip up there. Marius, the chalet host, will also pack it all up and ship everything down with our trash after we leave"

"Don't worry," whispered Marty. "I smuggled some good stuff to take in my pack."

"I can hear you, you know. You suck at whispering, Marty," said Andrew.

"Is it bourbon?" asked Jesse.

"C'mon you guys, let Liza finish," prompted Andrew, while the others continued to nudge and jostle each other like junior high schoolers.

"Everything else should be packed in your luggage. I've arranged to have the van moved to our final stay, at Lake McDonald Lodge, after we hit the trail. The staff there will deliver your bags to your rooms, so that when we arrive, you can freshen up for our last meal together. Any questions?" asked Liza.

Energy buzzed around the table, maybe from the multiple bottles of wine, but Liza was pretty sure it was because they were all ready for the adventure to begin. They had clearly mixed some oxygen into the fear and created excitement.

⋀ It's Hard to Let Go

At 4:00 AM, Diane made the rounds, quietly knocking on each guest's door to make sure they were all up thirty minutes before the meeting time. Her gentle knocks were met with, "Yeah, I'm up" or, in a few cases, a quickly opened door revealing bright-eyed excitement.

Only Jesse had overslept and Diane actually had to pound on his door. She hated making that much sound with people sleeping in adjacent rooms, but the man's snores were actually audible beyond the door. "Glad I'm bunking with Liza," she thought. "His wife must be thrilled to have a few nights without that buzz saw rattling her brain."

When he yanked the door open, standing annoyed and disoriented in his boxers and socks, he looked surprised to see her.

"OK, good, you're up," she said. "Jesse, do *not* go back to bed!" she admonished. "Get in the shower so you're at least a little bit awake and meet us in the lobby in 20 minutes." She had shortened the time, just in case he hadn't actually packed last night as Liza had instructed.

"Good morning!" boomed Marty as each of them stumbled into the lobby.

"Inside voice, for God's sake, Marty. Even the birds aren't awake yet," grumbled Jim. Liza was always amused to discover who was and wasn't a morning person on the first day of a trip. Each looked quizzically at the others, seeing them in surprisingly different garb than they typically wore. They were wearing the

49

clothes they would live in for the next several days. It was an interesting mix of high-end gear and obviously well-loved favorites. Fortunately, every one of them had broken-in boots. "Thank God for small favors," thought Liza, gratefully hoping that she wouldn't have to use her medic training on hideous boot blisters, as she sometimes did with newbies.

It's really hard to totally step away even for just a few days

"I wasn't sure you'd have time to break in your boots," Diane said, pointing to Jesse's feet as he stumbled into the lobby, hair wet from his hasty shower.

"Didn't have to. I just had to dig these out of the basement. We used to backpack all the time when I was first out of college. It's just been years since there's been any time. I wondered if they'd even fit, but man they feel familiar. If that makes sense."

"Sure does," said Andrew.

"OK, everybody," said Liza. "Electronics go in this box. Laptops, Kindles, phones, whatever you've got." She indicated a large strongbox with a lock. "Send your last message to whomever you need to and let 'em know we're headed to the glacier and you'll be off the grid until Thursday."

"What? You've got to be kidding me!" said Jesse, clearly alarmed. "I can't go without my phone. I've got a business to run." Rob was also holding onto his phone, hoping Jesse would win this fight.

"Sorry, Jesse. In the box," said Liza.

"No way! You can't be serious."

"Jesse, I know you weren't on all the calls, but I told you this when we spoke and it was also in bold print in the instructions. I told you to make sure you let everyone back home know you were going to be totally off the grid for three days."

"Yeah, I know, but I didn't think you were serious. No one means 'without my phone' when they say they're going to be off the grid. That's just a bullshit thing people say when they don't want to respond to stupid emails."

"Well, I meant it. It's totally off the grid. There are restrictions on using the generator at the chalet, so there's no way to charge anything and this is a trip about being fully present." She saw Jesse's exasperated look. "They're serious about no electronics because it's a hassle to have people bugging them to turn on the emergency generator and then moping around and acting like asses when they hear no, *no*, NO!"

"Well I've got young kids—what if my wife needs to reach me?" He was grasping, on the edge of panic.

Dan and Diane exchanged a glance, wondering whether one of them should step in or whether they'd let Liza handle it. Diane motioned Dan to wait.

"Did you not leave her the emergency number that was on the instructions?"

"Yeah, but what about an emergency at my company? I mean ... Or what if I want to take pictures?" He was scrambling for a way. It would have been comical if he hadn't looked like he was actually going to start crying. He had begun to shake and was breathing quickly.

Liza said to the others, "You guys take your gear out to the van. I'll be there in a minute. Just leave your bags at the back door of the van and get in."

The group moved into the pre-dawn cool to the van in front of the lodge. The van's exhaust was spiraling into a sky filled with more stars than any of them had ever seen.

Once the others had left the lobby, Liza softened her tone and held out her hand for Jesse's phone. "Don't worry, it's gonna be alright. I used to be you, you know, but with a pager. Yeah, that's how long ago, right? I actually stood screaming on a beach in front of hundreds of strangers threatening to divorce my husband when he threw my pager in the ocean. He was so fed up with how I let my career derail every intimate moment we had, including that family vacation, that he grabbed it off my swimsuit. Yes, it was that bad: I actually had my pager clipped to my bikini and had refused to go in the water with my daughter because of it. But he threw it into the water, and while I stood there screaming at him, oblivious to my daughter's sobs, he scooped her up and walked into the surf with her. I stormed off to our room, grabbed my credit card and then demanded that the concierge find out where I could buy a new pager.

"That's how I met Diane. She came up next to me as I was waiting for a taxi to take me from this beautiful resort into a tiny foreign town to buy a pager to continue distracting me from everything that mattered. All she said was, 'Can I tag along?'

"I thought she was nuts, but what did I care. As the taxi pulled up, she slid in next to me. I was still fuming, but something about her calming non-judgmental approach had me pouring out my guts to her about how I didn't know how to find my way anymore, I was scared that some other executive at my company was going to beat me at my own game while I was 'wasting my time on some stupid beach.' I actually said that. When I heard myself and saw the look of care on her face, I fell apart. We ended up sitting at a pool bar at another resort for hours while she coached me back to life.

"Probably three mai tais in, she asked me to look around the pool area and tell me what I thought each person was feeling. Honestly, Jesse, it felt like the first time in ages that I'd even looked at anyone else's face. At first, I didn't even know what I was seeing. She helped me slow down and really *look*. And then I saw it. The desperate sadness in the face of a woman whose pretty hair and manicured nails were unseen by her husband, who was pacing inside, shouting into the telephone, instead of being with her. I'd seen that look on my own husband's face dozens of times. I'd missed what had been written on my own child's face while I was throwing a hissy fit over my pager, but I saw it in the face of a toddler at the pool that day when her mother said 'stop bothering me and go play.' It broke my heart."

She watched the fight flow out of him. "I don't know you Jesse, but I do know what it means to be too scared to step away from your business for even a little bit. Something made you decide to say yes when Marty asked you to come. Trust me, your business will survive, and you might just see something you didn't expect without that phone in your hand."

He sighed and handed over his phone. "Did you ever get the pager?"

"You must not know Diane at all, Mister, if you even have to ask!" She locked up the strongbox and as he carried it out to the van for her, she said, "All I can tell you is that I learned that it's never about what it looks like it's about. And for me, it wasn't actually about the pager, it was what I used the pager to cover up."

> It's never about what it looks like it's about

Jesse helped Liza Tetris the gear into the back of the van. She slammed the door and nodded for him to get in.

Diane was already in the front passenger seat, so he took the open seat beside Marty in the middle row, pulled the door shut behind him and buckled in. Marty gave him a nod as Liza put the van in gear. They headed around the circular drive toward the road that would take them to the glacier.

It was quiet in the van, except for the occasional snore from someone in the back.

Both Marty and Jesse were awake, each lost in his own thoughts as the van rumbled through the still pre-dawn. The landscape around them was black, although they knew there was so much out there.

"It's hard letting go," said Marty in a raspy morning voice.

The younger man nodded. "It's OK, it's just a phone."

"Yeah, that too. But I meant, it's hard letting go of your baby," replied Marty, his voice low as the others slept. "I know I've made the right decision. Dan's a great guy and, to be honest, there was no way I could've taken the company to where it is without his help. It's just ..." He paused, trying to let the words filter up in his brain, "it's kind of all I've ever known."

In the dark, Jesse nodded. "Yeah."

"Even though I've done all this work—I mean, Marjorie and I are ready, but sometimes I wonder what it will be like when the day comes that I'm not there, at work. Early on, Diane asked me a question: 'Marty, what does work provide?' To tell you the truth, the only answer I had at the time was 'money.' But that chick kept asking, 'and what else?' Bit by bit, other answers started bubbling up. Stuff I didn't even know that I was getting from work."

"Like what?" asked Jesse, grateful that this conversation was happening in the dark; he didn't want anyone seeing his face. Because it scared him to think about letting go, turning his company over to someone else, even though he knew it was time, even though he knew this was the way to cash out and make sure his family was taken care of.

He was scared about a lot of things, and he felt stupid for feeling scared. And there was no one to talk to about it. He'd tried once, with his best friend. Jesse had told him, "I don't know what I'm going to do with myself once I sell." To which his friend had answered, "Boo hoo, dude, I wish I had your sad little $24 million problem." Jesse decided that day to forget about it, but it didn't go away, and now he also knew there really was no one he could talk to.

He was rightly scared about a lot of things

In fact, there were lots of things Jesse wanted to talk to someone about but didn't want to look like a spoiled brat with "rich people" problems, like being scared of not having made a difference with his life before it was over.

"Like … friendship," said Marty. "I know it sounds ridiculous, but after having spent more than thirty years in this business, the people feel like my friends. Not only my executives, but the vendors and the customers, other employees. I actually like them, well, a lot of them, anyway." His voice cracked, "and I'm embarrassed to say I don't really have a lot of friends anymore."

Jesse wondered whether the roughness in Marty's voice was sadness or because it was still so early. It also made him wonder if that's why Marty had brought his lawyer and his banker on this trip. Were they the only friends he had? Jesse's chest tightened as he realized that he would be hard pressed to find five guys to go on a trip like this with him. Not like his college days. Now it was pretty much his wife's friends or the parents of their kids they socialized with, when they socialized at all.

"I hear ya," Jesse replied. "I think it'd be hard to not talk to my customers or my team anymore. So many of them are, like you said, like friends at this point in my life. What else? Stuff you got from work, I mean?"

"So now you're gonna be like her?" Marty teased, nodding his chin at the front of the van, where Diane was humming softly to the song on the radio. "A lot of things. Some of which I'm not even sure I would have noticed until she started me thinking. Like, a place to go during the day to get out of the house; simple as that. Or a sense that I'm contributing to my community. Or, and I'm not proud of this, but power and respect."

"I get that," said Jesse. "When I'm in my car and I hear an ad on the radio for my company, it seems stupid, but I feel like I get a little swagger. Well, sitting-down-driving swagger."

"Right! People look at you differently when you're someone. Once I was talking about this with Rob, and he said he can see the difference in how somebody looks at him when he says he's an attorney. Between us, I think it's one of the reasons he's still practicing. I mean, he doesn't need the cash, but I think the poor sucker has no idea what he's going to do when he retires. So he keeps on working, even though I know his wife complains to Marjorie that she's lonely and wishes he'd retire so they could travel while they're still healthy enough to do it. I've talked to him about working with Diane and he says he's getting it by osmosis. You know, he's brought her in to work with another guy he's representing who's been talking about selling but keeps putting it off. I've heard Diane call that O-MY! syndrome."

"Which is?"

"One more year!" chuckled Marty. "Apparently, there are people who go pretty far down the sale and then pull it back, saying they'll put the firm back on the market later, they just need one more year. I've heard Jim talking about how frustrating it is when business owners call him year after year, just to talk, and then never seem to think it's the right time to sell."

Jesse felt his face grow red and wondered if Marty could tell he had been thinking about pulling out of their talks about his company just a couple of weeks ago.

The two fell silently into their own thoughts, Jesse making a mental note to jot down some thoughts when he could about this conversation and look at what else his work provided for him beyond the money, since the money Dan had offered was more than enough to take care of his family. And that mattered a lot right now. There must be something else that was making him hesitate. He knew the price was right, they'd done the math, but he kept scaring himself, wondering if it was really going to be enough. Maybe what Liza said was true: it's never about what it looks like it's about. But then what *was* it about?

As if reading Jesse's mind, Marty said, "I know that's what was happening for me when I almost killed my own deal by telling Jim I needed more money than was on the table. I was scared to death that I'd drop dead as soon as I sold because it's the only place I actually felt alive. Turns out, I just needed to figure out where I'd get all that other stuff I'd been getting from work but didn't realize I was getting."

"How'd you do that?"

"She's got her ways, my friend. Just wait, you'll see," said Marty.

Jesse wasn't exactly sure what he felt about Marty's last statement. Excitement? Fear about what he had gotten himself into by coming on this trip? And then he realized the van was turning into a big parking lot.

⋀ A Leap of Faith

There were several dozen cars in the parking lot of what was revealed to be the Logan Pass Visitors' Center.

Jesse was surprised to hear someone say it was thirty-eight degrees as he walked with Dan toward the restrooms. "That's pretty damned cold!" said Jesse.

"Yeah. Makes me glad I actually packed my gloves and woolies," said Dan. "I thought it seemed nuts when I saw those on the list and was going to skip them. I mean, I'd been looking at the temperatures on Weather.com for the last two weeks and it said it was in the seventies during the day and the fifties at night. But then my wife reminded me that I was looking at the temperatures for the lodge. I didn't particularly like her tone, but she was right when she asked me what temperature I thought glaciers lived in. I'm pretty sure she married me for my money and I married her for her brains!"

Jesse felt relaxed with Dan. Every time they'd been together, Jesse had felt like Dan would be the one, if there was anyone, he'd be able to hand the reins to. He hoped like hell that it wasn't an act and that he wasn't misjudging this guy, because his family's future would be in his hands if he went through with the deal.

The fog had rolled in deep and thick and, although other hikers were heading onto the trail, Liza told the group they'd have to wait. They'd made good time on the main road but she didn't want them to start until the fog lifted. Maybe not all the way, but certainly enough to let them be sure of their footing.

They were going to head up a trail called the Highline, across a part called the Garden Wall, a six-foot-wide trail that hugged the mountain cliff—with a steep canyon on the other side. They would be on this relatively flat but exposed trail for several miles, eventually connecting to the much steeper trail that would lead them to Granite Park Chalet, their home for the next two nights. Tomorrow they would trek out to the glacier from there.

It was just after what should have been sunrise, but exactly zero sunlight was getting through the clouds and fog. Although it was clear that the travelers were disappointed and antsy to get going, it was equally clear that Liza was not budging on her decision to wait.

Liza was handing out the boxed breakfasts to the men huddled around the van, and Diane was refilling coffee mugs while reminding everyone to make sure they stayed hydrated. Andrew liked that Diane was so unruffled by getting coffee. He interacted with plenty of strong professional women in his wealth management firm and lots of them would feel like they needed to make a show of not being the one getting coffee for anyone else, even if they were closest to the pot. He understood it, it had taken a lot for his sisters to climb their way up in their professions, but still, it was nice to see someone at ease with doing what needed doing and not constantly defending her position.

He first noticed her ability to put people at ease

It was that very ability to put others at ease that Andrew had first noticed when he met Diane. Marty had told him he was selling his company and had hired a banker to market the firm. Andrew hadn't known any of these people then, but he knew Marty trusted Jim to sell his company and that Marty's long-time attorney, Rob, was also involved. Most of the time Andrew didn't get that involved in the process until after the sale, when he began managing the proceeds. He always wanted to play a more active role, because often, he learned too late that they could have made better decisions to save his clients big chunks of tax. But he had always wondered whether it would look pushy to ask to be included in the deal process.

He had known Marty and Marjorie for a decade and knew that the company was their largest asset. It had seemed to him like they had a plan for what to do when they retired and they'd run various Monte Carlo simulations to make sure they'd have enough to live a long time and still leave money for their kids, even after long-term care, if they needed it.

It had been a surprise when Marty told him that he'd almost killed his own deal when Marjorie said she didn't want to do the sailing thing Marty had been yapping about. At the time, Marty hadn't told him that the deal had really fallen apart out of fear. Likely even Marty didn't know that at the time, Andrew now realized. All Andrew heard was that Marty had upped the price and that things had spiraled out of control.

Then Marty told Andrew he'd hired some kind of coach and invited Andrew to attend a meeting of all of his advisors. To say he was skeptical would have been an understatement. But, if for no other reason than his client asked him to attend and there was a lot at stake for the assets his firm was managing, Andrew had gone to the meeting.

The fog was getting heavier and what had been a gentle mist was turning into a steady drizzle. Liza suggested the group take cover in the visitors' center to wait for the weather to improve. It didn't surprise anyone when Jesse asked Liza if he could grab his phone from the strongbox since they were just going to be sitting around doing nothing anyway. Liza had no intention of indulging Jesse's numbing behavior and her face showed it. He shrugged. "Whatever."

Andrew thought Jesse's response was akin to what his sixteen-year-old daughter would have said, but imagined that it was hard for him to find his footing in this group given that he knew no one other than Dan and Marty prior to joining the trip. He actually thought Jesse was brave to have agreed to come on such a trip and told him so as the two took their newly refilled coffee mugs across the parking lot toward the visitors' center. The driz-zle was now turning to sleet in the near-freezing temperatures.

"Yeah, I guess. Thanks for saying so, though," said Jesse. "And by the way, I'm not usually such an ass about needing my phone. I'm a little anxious because I haven't really been away from my business before for this long, and … well, I don't al-ways know what to say. It seems like you guys all have a groove together and I kind of feel like the fifth wheel."

"I get it, Jesse," Andrew said as he pulled open the door to the visitors' center, letting Jesse go in first. "It's funny; I was just standing there thinking about the first time I met the rest of these guys. Doing something outside your comfort zone can rock anybody."

"So you weren't always part of this group?"

"Nope. I've managed Marty's investments for about ten years, but it was right after he met Diane that he asked me to come to an 'all-hands' meeting, I think he called it. That's where I met the other guys. Oh, and Karen, his accountant, was there, too. She and I had spoken on the phone a number of times, but we'd never met."

"Right, she's the one who couldn't come and that's why I'm here," offered Jesse, leaning against one of the massive log pillars supporting the roof.

"Right. I guess her father-in-law is dying."

"Mm-hm," said Jesse, his mouth a tight line.

"Anyway, it was one of the most unusual meetings I've ever been part of," continued Andrew. "I thought we were going to talk about the terms of the deal, maybe some financial details. I came prepared to talk about what Marty needed to get from the business to be able to retire. I had spreadsheets, charts, the whole nine. And then she starts talking about fears and …"

"Oh this, right?" said Jesse, smiling as he interrupted Andrew and held up his hand and made the fist brain, the way Diane and Marty had shown him on the train.

"Exactly! So you've seen it already?" Andrew asked, laughing.

"Yeah, it kind of blew my mind. Oo—nice one, me. She really did that whole thing in the meeting? With all you guys?"

"Yep. And, it was pretty interesting to observe the different reactions around that conference table, let me tell you. A bunch of high-powered deal professionals all making the brain fist; brain fist ... thing."

"The girly fist, Marty calls it," piped in Jesse.

"I know, and my girls would sock you for calling it that if they heard you, but it is the perfect visual to remind me that the lizard is supposed to stay tucked in for me to make good decisions. You know, at first I thought it was totally nutty, big-time flaky, but as I listened, it did kind of make sense and I started seeing lightbulbs going on in the other guys' heads, too. And I'll be darned, but I started to use it a bit in the way I interacted with my wife and my kids, and my staff and my clients. It **It explains why smart people can act like scared kids** made total sense how sometimes I'd be talking sense to a client and they'd be blabbering nonsense back to me, no matter how many times I explained something to them. Once I started to realize that when the person I was talking to was offline emotionally," he popped his fist open, fingers splayed, "nothing I could say was going to get through.

"It explained why smart people would come to my office to talk about their investments and behave like scared little kids," Andrew continued, "or do crazy stuff that totally undermined their retirement strategy, like blowing the money on some wacked-out thing."

Dan walked up to them and said, "Hey are you showing Jesse your lizard, Andrew? I thought we talked about that, man" smirking at his own humor. Andrew gave a small embarrassed smile as he turned his flipped-out fist brain into a waving hand.

Jesse took the bait. "I ain't scared, Dan. Marty already showed me his on the train, but mine is bigger!"

The men's rowdy laughter made Diane smile. Marty clearly wanted to get over there and hear what the joke was, but Diane put her hand on his arm. "Let Jesse find his way with Dan and Andrew. It's a good sign that he's laughing. It means he's starting to feel more comfortable and we want that vibe as we set out on the trail."

"Yeah, it's the first time I've actually seen him smile. Something is going on in that fella's head."

"I think so, too," agreed Diane. "He'll talk about it when he's ready. No reason to pry his lid off, that'll just scare him and he'll lock down even more. Relax and stop trying to figure him out; just enjoy this trip." She smiled and patted his arm again, returning her gaze to the two-story window being steadily pelted with sleet.

Jesse turned to Dan, "So you know this whole thing?"

"Sure do! We couldn't make sense of what happened when Marty suddenly demanded a boat-load more cash for his business. I could sense he was starting to get cold feet but we couldn't get a bead on what was going on, then bam, he was out. Stopped returning calls, went totally off the rails. Nothing we tried got him back to the table or back to the terms we'd already agreed on. Then Jim said he'd heard this gal speak at a conference. Called herself 'The Seller Whisperer.' I thought that was a bit much but figured it was worth a try. We had nothing to lose. So Jim brought her in."

"Did I hear my name?" said Jim, walking up to the others. "Geez, it's coming down out there. At first I was ticked off that Liza was letting a little fog and drizzle keep us off the trail, but I've gotta say I'm glad I'm not out there right now soaked to my skivvies on a slippery trail above a ravine."

"Yeah, me too," said Rob, joining the group as they stood looking out at tourists running for the cover of the visitors' center, rain jackets and brochures ridiculously perched over their heads but getting drenched anyway.

"I was telling Jesse that agreeing to come on this trip without really knowing us was like the leap of faith we all took in that first meeting with Diane," said Andrew.

"Too true," said Jim. "I saw how you guys were smirking and doodling on your pads as she did that whole 'here's your brain' thing."

The others nodded and Rob said, "Yeah, in fact I was thinking you'd lost your marbles bringing in this chick, Jim. Like, when was the group hug coming, you know? And then gradually, I realized she was doing the job that you and I had tried to do: she was talking Marty off the ledge and helping cooler heads prevail, so we could actually focus on the deal and finally make some progress."

"Mm-hm," said Jim. "We joke that we're all part psychologist when dealing with jacked-up sellers," he nodded to Jesse and said, "no offense man," then continued, "but I'll tell you, not having to do that and being able to just focus on the deal has been a Godsend."

"Amen," added Rob. "I didn't even realize how much time and energy I had been wasting trying to keep my clients sane and moving forward until I started using Diane on other deals. It means that when I see a client's number on my cell, I'm not rolling my eyes thinking, 'what now?' Come to think of it, I'm taking way fewer of those weekend and late-night crazy calls."

"Yeah, because they're calling her instead!" added Jim.

"Wait," said Jesse. "Isn't that the job of the banker on the deal? To handle the stuff that comes up and keep the deal moving? I mean, I thought that's what I'm paying the big bucks to that guy for."

"Sure," said Jim. "It's the job of the banker or the broker to keep the deal moving. That's not moving off your intermediary's plate, but what is is the other stuff, the times the seller gets ticked off about something and starts railing. That stuff, Diane handles."

"Jesse, listen, you haven't had a lot of friction in your deal," offered Dan.

"Yet!" chimed in Jim and Rob, clinking their empty coffee mugs together.

"Knock it off, knuckleheads," Dan said. He turning back to. "But think about that first time we asked for financials and you got snippy."

Jesse made a face.

"Listen, it happens. But what I've learned from Diane is that it's normal. Apparently, it's shame and fear. And until I realized that, I would have just pushed you harder and got in your face about it, thinking it was a sign that you had something to hide."

"Yeah … that wouldn't have worked," said Jesse.

"Exactly, but what I've seen is that when we've had Diane involved, she helps to normalize all of that predictable emotion and gives our sellers a safe place to process it, without it spilling all over the deal and without them looking like whining wimps," continued Dan.

"And, much as I hate to admit it, she does the same thing for the rest of us, too," said Rob. "I'm absolutely fed up with the shenanigans of opposing counsel on a deal we're doing right now and, rather than pound on the other attorney like I'd like to, Diane has helped me see that that's my amygdala on fire and there's a better way to approach the situation. And because she's in the deal, she's able to help calm the emotions on all sides."

Unaddressed emotions kill deals

"Yes—our close ratio is way higher than it was last year," added Jim. "It's counterintuitive to me as a banker to slow things down. Before we started using her, I would have said 'time kills all deals' but now I realize that it's … how does she put it? 'Unaddressed emotion kills all deals.' I've gotta admit that that was above my pay grade until I got a better handle on what it means and how to do some of it. Honestly, it wasn't until she helped me see that my own fear of losing the commission was causing me to chase Marty."

"Ahh! The Island-Wave-whatever thing," interrupted Jesse.

"Uh-huh. The harder I chased him, the faster he ran. I had no idea I was causing some of it. It made me realize that I don't need to chase more deals, I need to be able to help the sellers in the ones I'm in to feel more settled so *they* can close." Jim continued, "I used to get calls from sellers all the time. They'd tell me they were ready to go, I'd put in a bunch of work and then they'd flake out and tell me they needed 'one more year' whatever the hell that meant—and then they'd resurface, only to flake out again."

Jesse hoped his face wasn't burning and that Dan couldn't tell he'd been thinking about pulling out just a couple of weeks ago.

"I know," said Dan. "We used to wonder what was going on after we'd put a bunch of money into courting a seller and they'd bail. Now we get it, it's fear, and we started to see how we were triggering a bunch of it, too. Diane has been helping us to find other ways to deal with our own deal anxiety so we're not leaking it all over the good guys whose companies we actually do want to buy."

"Well, it helped once you stopped punching every seller in the nose and strong-arming them," nodded Jim. "That guy you had as your lawyer on the deal with Marty nearly killed it again just when we pulled it out of the fire."

Dan nodded slowly, "Yeah, that was a mistake on our part. When he refused to come to that meeting with Diane, I pressured him to go because you told me it was important, Jim. But it was clear from the beginning that he wasn't buying it. Called it a pile of crap. I thought he'd come around, but every time I wanted to take a more measured approach to how we were dealing with Marty and bring Diane into our conversations about strategy, he'd have none of it. It was like he was just getting more belligerent and looking for ways to prove she was wrong about what would help to keep Marty engaged and lessen the fire in the deal. We managed to get it to a close, but no thanks to his ham-handed approach. Without Diane, I think we would have had a really tough time getting Marty to stay on for the past year."

Dan was shaking his head. He turned to Jesse. "But don't worry, Jesse, we switched attorneys after Marty's deal. A little bit of friction in any deal is normal and natural, but conflict for the sake of showing someone who's boss serves no purpose. In our deals, we work hard to own it when our ego's getting the better of us and to 'tame that lizard.' The legal team we're using now is totally on board with this approach to understanding the emotional part of our deals and how we can better move toward what we're all trying to achieve: a happy buyer *and* a happy seller." Dan was worried the talk about how harsh his attorney had been would scare Jesse off, and he could already sense that Jesse had been concerned about something he couldn't put his finger on.

"Thanks, Dan, I was wondering about that as I heard you telling how rough it was for Marty. I mean, I gotta say, my lawyer told me not to come on this trip. She said it was just a ruse for you and Marty to pump me for information and squeeze me with it later." His face turned red as he realized he hadn't meant to say that out loud and didn't want Dan to think he didn't trust him, when in fact Marty and Dan had almost seemed too good to be true. Skepticism about what they'd really be like if he closed the deal was one of the things that had made him pull back.

"Jesse, Marty asked you to come on this trip because Karen couldn't come and Marty and I genuinely thought we would all enjoy each other's company. *Not* so we could pump you for information or trick you into thinking we're something we're not. It's natural for your attorney to want to protect you. And we don't need to talk about business at all. In fact, I'm guessing that if Diane catches us, she'll give us all a whupping!"

"More likely Liza," said Jesse, "the phone police!"

They all laughed.

Rob added, "As natural as it is for your attorney to warn you about over-sharing on this trip, I want you to hear it from me: that's her fear showing. Before I started doing this work with Diane, as an attorney I would have said the same thing. I would have tried to convince a client like you not to go and I'd warn them to be guarded. But now I do it differently. I tell my clients the risks of things, without needing to scare their pants off, and I help them to make reasoned decisions to evaluate those risks, rather than trying to paper every deal to death just to make sure that a client doesn't come back on me. That's what it's about, not psychoanalysis and inner feelings and hugging everyone."

Jim said to Jesse, "On the deal side, we call that 'churning,' when a lawyer keeps racking up the hours, fighting over every little nonsensical thing, making change after change after change, just because they can. Meanwhile, the parties get angrier and more frustrated, and the only one who's winning is the attorney who's racking up more billable hours, even if the deal dies a slow, painful death for everyone else."

"Very nice, Jim, I can see you hold my brethren in high esteem!" said Rob.

"Not you, Rob, but you know what I'm saying is true. The more fear there is in a deal, the higher the fees, the longer it takes and the worse toll it takes on everyone, including the professionals," replied Jim. "And the worst part is that it doesn't have to be that way. We've proven that in the different way we've been doing deals since we started working with Diane."

"Jim's making a good point," Rob said. "I'm not saying that's what your attorney is doing, Jesse—I don't even know her. But, you seem like a smart fellow, with a good gut and a good head. Remember, whatever you decide to do with your deal, you don't have to make it happen in a way that destroys you or the other side. There are choices and Jim is right that being able to understand what drives that impulse is an important part for all of us in any deal now that we know that's what's going on.

There *is* a better way

Believe me, I understand that the kinder, gentler touchy-feely approach seems weird and is wildly uncomfortable at first. We're not trying to brainwash you.

"But enough of that for now," Rob continued. "The focus of this trip is to celebrate with Marty as he wraps up his final year with Dan and his team. In fact, where is he?"

Jesse was wondering why Dan hadn't had Diane work with him yet, but before he could ask if Dan planned to, Dan said, "Look alive, fellows, Diane and Liza just got out of their chairs and are headed this way with Marty. We'd better not look like we were talking business."

"How 'bout them Mets?—"

"—those Cubs," said Jim and Rob in unison, cracking each other up as Liza approached.

"Looks like it's clearing," she said. "We'd better get a move on."

⋀ Slow but Steady

Even with her sunglasses on, the sunshine felt especially bright to Diane after the hours they'd spent in the visitors' center. They were ready to go!

Liza tightened the straps on her pack so it rode low on her hips; it towered above her head. She called, "Everybody circle up. We're going to follow that path," pointing to the right of the visitors' center.

"Several of you have asked if we'll still make it to the chalet, given the long delay because of the weather. The answer is yes, I've allowed plenty of time in our schedule and it's better that you take your time than rush. It's not a race. The clouds are breaking apart and the sun is a good sign for the trip ahead. Two reasons to take your time, OK? First, we don't want you slipping and plunging down the ravine—that *will* make us late, right, when we have to rescue you. And it's a long way to the nearest hospital."

Looks of concern were exchanged.

"That's not going to happen, just take your time. And the second reason is that you're going to have the most amazing view across the valley and over part of Going-to-the-Sun Road. You won't want to miss checking that out. It's something that visitors who stay in their cars don't get to see. If we're lucky, we might spot bald eagles and maybe even mountain goats or big-horn sheep along the way today. Speaking of animals, remember what I told you about bears. Do not approach, do not feed, do *not* run. Make noise." Seeing more concerned faces, she added, "But we are highly unlikely to see one, given that other hikers have been up today to scare them off.

"I've got extra water and snacks. Stay hydrated and ask for what you need along the way. Waiting until you're thirsty or hungry is too late on a hike like this. We'll stay mostly together and don't worry, no one will be left behind. I've got a camera and I'll snap some shots of you along the way. Everybody ready?"

And with that, the band of eight was off.

Jesse and Jim were tall and their strides seemed to mean that they were always creeping up on the others and crowding them. They were also the least patient of the group and found it hard to contain their desire to push the others to go quicker. At one point, when he had been stuck behind Marty and Rob, Jesse realized his sighs of frustration were audible, and he became aware that he didn't want to seem ungrateful for this experience that Marty had generously offered him. The older men seemed to struggle just a little to build a rhythm and their packs, though lighter than Jesse's, seemed uncomfortable on their backs. He wondered what it would feel like to be that age and undertake a journey like this.

Liza had noticed Jesse and Jim moving faster and suggested they go a little ahead, but cautioned them to wait at the junction of the next trail for the rest of the group. As Jesse and Jim settled into a companionable silence, covering the trail more quickly than the others, Jim was often the one who would suggest pausing, taking in the scenery and having a drink of water or a bite to eat.

Jim thought about how often he rushed through other parts of his day or, in fact, his life. As he stood munching on an apple, wondering exactly how far he was seeing into the distance, he wondered what it would be like to be able to have this kind of view of where his career was headed. It always seemed that he was on a manic push to close the next deal and the next. Sure, he was aware of the need to meet more sellers, to fill his pipeline, and he considered that prospecting as a kind of relationship skill. It had never re-ally occurred to him before to continue to stay in touch with sellers whose deals he had closed. Yet this past year, since he'd closed with Marty, it seemed as if the concept of customer relationship management had taken on a totally different meaning.

He wanted to retire happily

Instead of trying to rush sellers to get ready to sell their businesses, he had started slowing down to get to know them better, earlier in the process. He and Andrew had spent a fascinating evening talking with Diane, about a month after Marty's deal closed, about how they could find out sooner the kinds of landmines that had first blown up Marty's deal. She helped them look at how their own discomfort about what they would do when *they* retired and how *they* would step out of their careers made it hard for them to relate deeply to the fears that their clients were facing, and how their worries made them more likely to accept surface answers like "travel and golf" when they asked what a client would do after selling their business.

Much as he hated to admit it, Jim was terrified of what it would be like to stop working and he cringed each time he heard himself say the same kind of things he heard from owners he knew should be selling but weren't. Like the seventy-nine-year-old who said he wanted to work another ten years. Or his buddy who had been a senior executive at a Fortune 500 company, retired, and then became a business broker at sixty-two after only six months of traveling with his wife, joking that he had "flunked retirement." Jim admitted to himself that he was worried he, too, might flunk retirement.

He and his wife had barely survived the crisis in their marriage when the twins went to college two years ago. That empty nest had made it even more obvious that they had lost their connection and, when he was honest, it was one of the reasons he had started to take on more and more deals and his travel schedule had crept up again. It was easier to say they weren't doing anything together because of his hellish schedule. That was better than the truth he feared—that she didn't want to be with him any more than he wanted to be with her. Maybe that was the reason she didn't complain anymore about how often he was away.

They had planned for it financially, but had they planned for it emotionally?

Suddenly he didn't feel like swallowing any more of that apple and tossed the remainder over the edge, enjoying how it disappeared into the tree cover below. Kind of like staying busy covered up the fear that if he stopped working, they'd divorce and he'd lose half of everything he'd worked so hard to build. He could hear the voices of the others coming up the trail behind them and he didn't feel like talking right now. It made him glad he was hiking with Jesse, who seemed to have drifted into his own bit of melancholy as they'd stood looking out at the view. Jim wondered what the hell was wrong with him. Here he was, on the trip of a lifetime, a spectacular view laid out before him, feeling disappointed in the life he was living. Honestly, he was glad to just keep moving and, like in his marriage and with his career, he hoped that what he was worried about wouldn't catch up to him. If he just kept moving.

Jim wiped his hands on his pants and nodded to Jesse and the two moved on toward the intersecting trails.

Andrew didn't mind bringing up the rear with Marty and Rob. He was used to hiking at a slower pace and knew that if you went too quickly, you could miss a wildlife sighting. He was glad Liza had made them leave their electronics behind. With headphones blaring music or a podcast into your ears you'd never hear a rare bird call. In fact, he was enjoying the sound of their footfalls. He liked the frequent stops for the older guys to catch their breath. Rather than wait until either of them was winded, he had taken it upon himself to be the one who pointed out a sight or suggested they pause. He had a genuine fondness for Marty and was grateful Marty had asked him to come along. To Andrew, that was a signal that he had become one of Marty's truly trusted advisors.

Andrew had hiked a lot with his grandfather when he was young and it had instilled in him a love for nature that he had shared with his daughter when she was young. Now that she was a teenager, she had less interest—in nature or in him. Every time he or his wife took her on a college tour, it made him painfully aware that they would soon be empty nesters. Sure, they had planned for it financially, but had they planned for it emotionally? He saw this play out with his clients way too often, although he hadn't quite been able to name it before. They would set a wealth goal and, inevitably, as soon as they came within sight of it and the freedom it represented, they would move the finish line, sometimes even adding a zero to the number. One of his clients who already had $20 million in investments repeatedly asked Andrew whether it would be enough. Never mind that the couple had never spent more than $200,000 in a year, all in. He hadn't quite understood how to break through that cycle with his clients until the experience he'd been through with Marty.

Marty and Marjorie lived a moderate lifestyle and the money he had been set to bring in from the sale of his business was more than they could ever spend, even if they both lived to be a hundred. That was why everyone, including Andrew, had been stunned when Marty said he needed so much more. Andrew had had another client, who was in the middle of a deal to sell his four-franchise business for a tidy sum, tell him that during heart bypass surgery three weeks before the closing, God had told him that he was meant to keep the business and he had been saved for just that reason. God? Had told him that?!

It became obvious that the real issue that this client and Marty and, hell, even Andrew, faced was that as long as they kept working they could pretend they were immortal. Why this hadn't occurred to him before was dumbfounding to Andrew, but he hadn't quite known how to have that conversation, especially since he didn't really want to have it with himself. But he knew he needed to find a way when, that night he was out with Diane and Jim, she had told them both that their unwillingness to face the issue themselves was impairing their ability to have the conversations with their clients and that it was one of the reasons neither was having the kind of regular engaged success with clients that they wanted to: they both wanted to fill the role of "trusted advisor" but felt they were often shut out and always ended up being subjected to fee pressure. Someone else would promise to manage a client's money for a quarter-point less and they'd bolt. Andrew knew she was right, that it was about finding the courage to talk about mortality and the elusive topic of legacy that was missing from the way he served his clients. He knew he kept skirting these issues because he didn't know how to deal with them for himself either. He hoped this trip would help him find some answers.

When all eight hikers had arrived at the marker where the Garden Wall portion of the Highline Trail ended, Liza made sure everyone's water was topped up and the bags of trail mix and dried fruit were handed around.

Marjorie had been a miser with the sweets while Marty was trying to drop the pounds for this trip and his doctor had been on his case about salty snacks because of a rise in his blood pressure during the sale process. It had gone back down as the deal got back on track, but Marjorie had still kept watch, so Marty especially loved the mix of sweet and salty in the trail mix and he gobbled handful after handful, cramming his mouth like the chipmunks they had watched at one of their rest stops.

Marty had hoped to have seen more wildlife by now, but he also knew he might have missed plenty of things because, other than the times they had stopped for breaks and to take in the view, he had mostly been keeping his focus on the trail. Liza was right; it had been slippery in spots. He didn't want to trip and knock his front teeth out or plunge into the ravine.

Marty had been glad for Rob's company on the trail. They were well matched in pace and Rob hadn't wanted to talk about business. He could tell some of them still had their minds on what they had left behind. It made him grateful for the train ride. Diane had been right that the slower pace would allow him to ease into the trip and enjoy more of it than if they had flown, with all the rushing and impatient waiting that entailed these days. He was secretly relieved when she asked whether he would like her to fly to Chicago and take that first part of the journey with him.

He wouldn't have asked for that extra time from her, she had already spent so many hours with him and Marjorie over the past year, helping them adapt to the changes that were happening, and he knew Diane would continue to help them even after his last day at the company. They had talked about how each new step would bring its own uncertainty, even when it was something he was looking forward to. Marty genuinely enjoyed spending time with her, liked the way unexpected topics opened whenever they talked, liked how she helped him think about things in ways that he didn't seem to find for himself, especially when life was busy or he was feeling stressed. Marjorie thought the idea of him going by train was a good one, too. In fact, he had been surprised to learn that she'd always wanted to go on a train trip since she had read *Murder on the Orient Express*. Maybe he'd ask Liza to recommend a trip he and Marjorie could take that would make her dream come true, too.

"C'mon Marty, let's go," said Andrew. He was waiting to make the trek up the trail to the chalet with Marty. This part of the trail was steeper and tree covered. It was like going through a tunnel. Marty was surprised there were still trees this high up, this close to the glacier. But these were what kind? Spruce? Some kind of evergreen. Liza would know; he'd ask her when they got to the chalet. He had so many questions, even with all the months of research he had done, reading every night and spouting so many facts that Marjorie just smiled indulgently every time he said, "Hey, did you know that ..."

"I like that guy more every time I spend time with him," Marty thought as he started up the trail ahead of Andrew, wiping the salt off his whiskers. He hadn't bothered to shave that morning, given that it felt more like night when they met in the lobby anyway. How long had it been since he hadn't shaved every single day? "Maybe," he thought, "I'll grow a beard when I retire. Hmm, retire? Yeah, retire," Marty said to himself, and was a little surprised at how he actually liked the sound of that.

"Want trek poles?" asked Liza as she came up beside them and offered the poles to Marty and Rob. "It'll make the incline more manageable."

"I will if you will," said Rob as he looked to Marty. The lawyer's face was bright red and covered in sweat and Marty could tell that the incline was steeper than either of them had thought it was going to be. Even using the incline feature on the treadmill at the gym hadn't prepared him for what it felt like right now. Of course, he reminded himself, he hadn't done his incline work *after* already hiking that many miles and getting up at oh-dark-something.

There's nothing like having someone you trust beside you

"Sure, unless of course, *you* want them," Marty said, turning to Andrew, who was also sweating but not like Marty and Rob. Andrew shook his head and smiled. Marty took the poles from Liza and thought, "How the hell is she still so chipper, and carrying that gigantic pack as if it's filled with cotton balls?"

He and Rob set off, determined to make it to the chalet without keeling over, kind of like how they had both made it to the end of the deal, even when he had thought he'd rather just sit down on a stump and call it quits. "There's nothing," thought Marty, "like having someone you trust beside you to make it through the uphill parts when things feel insurmountable." And, grateful as he was for the poles, which helped to steady him, he was aware that if he did stumble, Andrew was there at his back. With a bout of gratitude that seemed to give him strength, he thought, "I know that these people could have chosen to be anywhere right now and every one of them left work and family behind to come on this trip. With me. How lucky am I!" And then he smelled the unmistakable smell of Dinty Moore canned beef stew. How that memory popped into his mind he had no idea, and then he realized it must mean the chalet was just up ahead. Thank God. He realized for the first time that they were out of the woods and the sky had opened up above them, a blue like he had never seen.

⩕ Nourishing Trust

As Marty stepped off the trail and onto the stone walkway that led to the chalet, the rest of the group was applauding. Truly, he was proud of himself. He had completed something today that would have been unthinkable for him a year ago, when he was in the throes of the deal. Each one of his companions stepped forward to hug him, even Jesse, although it was more like the bro-hug he'd seen young guys give each other, awkward but still full of feeling. Marty had to say it felt like the best day of work he'd put in in a long time and his sweaty face told him he'd feel proud of this day for a long time.

Then he realized Liza was talking and he'd better pay attention.

"We'll meet for dinner inside the main lodge," she was saying. "If any of your stuff is wet, bring it into the lodge and dry it by the fire. It's a good communal setting and the conversation in the dining hall is usually pretty interesting. I think you'll enjoy it.

"So," she continued, "it's two to a room. Obviously, Diane and I are together and we'll take that room," she indicated the nearest cabin, "and the three right beyond are for you fellows. Up to you to choose your roomie, so grab a sleeping bag and we'll see you in a bit for some grub."

Jesse and Andrew were the first to grab their sleeping gear and head down the path to where the cabins were. Jesse thought the word "room" was too generous for what appeared to be tool sheds butted up against each other. It was conceivable that the main building could be deemed a "chalet" but who were they kidding with these? He was glad Marty had paid his way because otherwise he'd definitely be asking for a refund on the lodging. Then he caught himself and thought, "How did I become such a selfish, miserable loser?" remembering that he was lucky to have been included in such an adventure. He reminded himself to be grateful and enjoy the beautiful surroundings instead of constantly looking for what was wrong. That kind of thought had been pulling him out of his anger a lot lately, even though he'd tell anyone who asked that he had a hell of a lot to be angry about right now.

Because he figured they'd all be the same, Jesse pulled open the door to the cabin next to the one the girls had chosen. No sense in walking farther than he had to for the john. As he opened the door, he realized this was going to be even more rustic than he had imagined. The tiny room held stacked bunkbeds with impossibly thin, plastic-wrapped mattresses, one wooden chair and a table that held a metal bowl. "Sponge bath" flitted into his head. He noticed several wooden pegs pounded into the wall, four on either side of the table, just under the tiny window covered by a dingy cotton curtain.

He remembered there was no electricity as he reflexively reached for a light switch that wasn't there.

"Good thing you didn't bring your phone, huh?" Andrew said. Jesse couldn't tell if he had seen him looking around for an outlet just moments before. Was he just busting his chops? "Guess that's why she had us bring flashlights. And extra batteries."

"Top," called Jesse, tossing his sleeping bag on the upper bunk before hanging his pack on a peg and peeling off the sweat-soaked layers of clothes.

Rob and Jim took the next cabin, leaving Marty and Dan in the one farthest down.

Dan was soaping up the washcloth when he said to Marty, "What's up? You're awfully quiet."

"I don't know. I'm just kind of disappointed that these places aren't quite what I thought they would be. It sounds stupid, but do you think I look cheap for having us stay in this dumpy little place?" Marty asked

"Are you serious?" Dan lowered his voice, since realizing the walls were so thin that every conversation could be heard in the other rooms. "This trip is amazing, Marty. Every second of it. From the moment the van picked the guys and me up at the airport, last night's dinner. Liza. Even the fog this morning. It couldn't be more perfect. The whole time I was hiking today I was thinking about how lucky I am that you brought your company to me and that you trusted me enough to spend the past year digging in with me. When the deal nearly died, the fact you were able to come back to the table, to open the door again and let me in—that took guts. I had hoped we'd be able to find our way into a good working relationship and navigate the transition together. And to think that we're here, in this raw wild place together. Sharing a cabin. For God's sake, I'm standing here in my long johns talking to the man who was worried I was screwing him over a year ago.

"Can you even take in the trek we've made? Not just today across that freaking gorgeous wall and up that crazy-steep trail. But the one we've traveled this past year, pal. And tomorrow we're going to stand on the edge of a glacier together. I can tell you, there's not a single person on this trip, not even Jesse, who's wondering whether you could have made this a better trip. And, by the way, we're on the edge of a glacier, dude. Did you actually think there'd be a Ritz Carlton here?" joked Dan. "You're worried about looking cheap? Seriously? You look like George freaking Bailey, surrounded by people who would have paid more than you can imagine for the chance to see what we're going to see, and the fact we get to see it with you makes all of it sweeter.

"Nobody asks anyone to do what you've done, Marty. You've dug deep into the undergrowth in yourself and I've seen how it's changed you. And you got this raggedy pack of explorers to drop into that same uncharted territory and be vulnerable in ways no one else does in a deal. I don't know anyone else who's asked their goddamned deal team to help them celebrate the end of their earn-out and witness their dream coming true with them." Dan saw Marty relax, and saw an expression of gratitude on his face.

"So get out of here and boil your own wash water while I finish up and change my shorts. Even Diane wouldn't ask us to get *that* personal."

Coming back to the table took guts

As he stepped into the cold and pulled the door closed behind him, Marty thought, "I guess we have been on a journey together all this time. I hadn't realized that's what it was."

⋀ Dithering

Diane was chopping vegetables and adding them to the pot Liza was stirring when Jesse wandered into the kitchen, hoping to find something warm to drink. The temperature was falling rapidly as the sun dropped. "How long till dinner?" he asked, reaching around Diane and grabbing a chunk of carrot.

"Another half hour or so," answered Liza. It smelled earthy and he realized he was hungry. He asked, "Need help with anything?"

The two women exchanged a look of surprise with raised eyebrows that said, "Huh, you can never tell about some people." Jesse hadn't seemed like one who would pitch in.

"Sure," said Liza, "Wanna take over the chopping or make the cornbread?" nodding her head to the pile of blue and white boxes of Jiffy cornbread mix that were mounded on the counter beside Diane.

"Do I have to wear an apron?" He smirked, referring to the floral cotton apron Diane was wearing.

"Don't like flowers, Jesse?" she teased. "Surprised I wear an apron when I cook, or that I brought it with me on the trip?"

"Uh, both."

"There's a lot you don't know about me, Jesse, that might surprise you."

"Like what?" he asked, reaching for a box of mix.

"Don't forget," Liza said, "we're at altitude, so use those instructions on the box, OK?"

"OK. How many?"

"Use them all. I imagine everyone is going to be hungry and what we don't eat tonight will be good for tomorrow. They'll hold."

He was opening drawers and cabinets, looking for a mixing bowl and spoon. "Should I make muffins or cakes," he asked as he stood looking at the array of baking dishes.

"Which do you like?" asked Diane.

"Either I guess. Wait. No, muffins. I used to make these corn muffins with my grandma when I was a kid. We'd put actual corn kernels in them and then slather them with honey at the kitchen table." He fell suddenly silent.

Liza said, "That's a fun memory, Jesse. Is she still alive?"

"No, she died when I was eight. Colon cancer. All I remember is she had to wear that disgusting bag that stunk and ..." Diane looked up and saw his eyes squeezed shut.

"Then, muffins it is, Jesse. I saw a big plastic bear of honey in the dining room when I was making tea earlier."

"Oh, tea—that's what I originally came in for. I forgot," he said with unnatural brightness. "I'll get these in the oven and then I'll make some tea."

The three of them worked silently together except for the sounds of stirring spoons and chopping knives. Twenty minutes later, the others began filtering into the dining room.

"Just in time, gentlemen," said Liza, as Jesse pulled the cornbread from the oven. "Grab a bowl and get yourself some chili. Diane, can you put the muffins in that basket?"

"I'll do it," offered Jesse. Diane handed him the big metal bowl she had lined with a flowered cloth. "Tell me you didn't also bring this?"

"OK, I won't tell you," she smiled. Even roughing it deserved some gentle touches, in her view.

"Bean chili? Oh great!" Liza heard someone chortle behind her. And then the retort, "Don't pull the hood over your sleeping bag, buddy, you'll suffocate yourself." The group fell silent as spoons dipped into bowls.

After dinner was done and the dishes were washed, Marty's group settled in around the fire with Marius, the chalet host, and the other three hikers who were staying overnight. Liza had been right, the nights got cold up here. Marius told them that this late in the season he was happy to have such a small group of travelers to spin tales with. Apparently, only two weeks ago, every cabin had been booked and there were more through hikers making the trek up to the glacier and down to the visitors' center, although they were more experienced hikers.

Marty's group wasn't up to an out-and-back trek—it had been more than enough to cover almost ten miles today. Marty couldn't imagine going another couple of miles farther to the glacier and then covering that whole distance again, just to get in the van and drive somewhere else to sleep. He was grateful that Liza had mapped out the trip the way she had. He didn't want to be rushed when he got to see the massive sheet of ice.

Marty heard Andrew telling the other group of hikers about how this was Marty's big hurrah after selling his company. The two men and a woman looked impressed and Marty felt his chest swell a little with pride. He felt a sense of warmth for his traveling companions, and seeing them lounging here, bodies warming by the fire, some with their boots off and socked feet propped up, filled his heart.

Marty noted that the woman had elbowed her husband as if she knew he had something to ask. Marjorie had done that more than he liked in their married life. He always wondered how women knew when their husbands had something on their mind and just needed a little prod to let it out.

The man, who looked to be about seventy, cleared his throat and asked, "How did you finally decide to sell?"

Marty said, "It wasn't so much that I decided, it just seemed that it kept coming up for me. Like maybe I should think about it. But then, things would get busy again at work and it would kind of drift back out of view."

He patted his wife's hand. "Luisa has been pushing me to sell and do more of this," he said, waving his hand to take in the rustic scene. "We typically get out for a week every year, sometimes two, if we're lucky." His wife made a little snort. "OK, to be honest, this is the first week I've taken off in a couple of years."

"Try ten years," chimed in his wife, "and only because I told him we had to do something before we were too old to do anything. Our grandson here is heading off to start his MBA at Harvard in a couple of weeks," she said with pride, although the young man looked embarrassed.

"Anyway, his dad and I don't really talk anymore," said the man. At the mention of the friction between his father and grandfather, the young man excused himself and went into the kitchen to make himself another cup of hot chocolate. "Well," continued the man, "I'd always hoped I'd get to do something like this when I turned the reins over to him and retired. Sadly, my son wanted nothing to do with my business, so I guess I've just kept working." He lowered his voice and said to the group, "Frankly, I'm kind of holding on till the boy graduates in a couple of years. And I figure, I'm not getting any younger—I might not actually be able to do this kind of a trip with him then. So we," he clasped his wife's hand and shook it gently, "figured we'd best do it now."

"Otherwise I doubt I could have gotten him to even take this week off," she added. "But it's been amazing. We should have done it sooner."

"I'm hoping he'll want to take over when he finishes school," the man continued. "I've even met with my lawyer to talk about leaving the company to him in my will, so he can have it if I die before he's finished school." His head hung down, not noticing the worried looks that were passing between the advisors who had been listening to his story. His wife let go of his hand and put her hand on his back, "We'll figure it out, honey. Give it some more time."

Diane noticed that the young man had slipped out the back kitchen door and she followed, looking to retrieve something from her room.

He was leaning against the stone chalet wall, steam rising from his cup, when Diane came out the door. They nodded to each other and stood for a minute or two, in awe at the star-filled sky. At home she always slipped out at night to stand in her bare feet in the cool grass of her front yard, looking up at the stars before she tucked in at night. It made her feel connected to something bigger.

He sipped from his cup. "Was my grandpa going on about how he's hoping I'll take over his company when I finish my MBA?"

"Yeah, how did you know?" she asked.

"Easy. We never talk about it, him and me. But ever since my dad told him he wasn't joining the family business, it's like he's pinned all his hopes on me. No one ever even asked me if I want to. I'm just caught in this battle between my dad, who thinks I shouldn't, and my grandparents, who assume I will."

"What do *you* want?" she asked.

"What does it matter?" he replied. "No matter what I choose, I'm screwed. If I go into the business, my parents will disown me. If I don't, I lose any chance of staying connected with my grandparents." He paused, "It's only since I went away to college that I even get to see them again. Once they had their blow-up over the business and stopped talking to each other, my grandparents cut my parents off. And in retaliation, my parents wouldn't let them see me. My mom sent their letters and even my Christmas presents back unopened.

"I've been working for the past three years and we talk on the phone and stuff, but never about the business or what I'm going to do after I finish grad school. But I can tell they have their hopes set on it and I get the sense he's desperately hanging on. I probably shouldn't be telling you any of this since it's kind of private, but I don't think the business is really doing well.

"My parents think I'm on a trip with my college roommates this week. And it sucks to not be able to send them photos. I know I'll have to edit the entire story when I get back home." His shoulders slumped and he sighed deeply.

"Sounds like a terrible bind," Diane said. "What do you think you'll do?" she asked.

"I don't know. I think they thought this trip would sway me their way, although sometimes I think they've already decided for me, just like my parents think they have in the other direction. Maybe I'll just continue on after my MBA and get a PhD and continue to avoid the whole thing even longer." His voice cracked, and he downed the rest of the hot chocolate. "At least that way no one will be disappointed with me."

Diane continued on to her room and pulled the small bag of marbles out of her backpack. She was glad she had thought to tuck them in, even though at one point when they were rubbing against her spine on the trail she had wondered what she'd been thinking.

When she reentered the chalet, the conversation had shifted to what they would see tomorrow when they went to the glacier. The young man and his grandparents were going to walk the trail to the edge of the glacier tomorrow and then head back down. They had only one more night in the park before they went their separate ways.

Diane said she wanted to try something with the whole group. "Are you game?" Some people shrugged; others said, "Sure," their curiosity piqued. She untied the gold-colored string at the top of the little red velvet bag and, handing it to Rob on her left, she said, "I want you each to choose a marble. There's plenty in the bag and they're all different. Choose one that calls to you." She saw Marty reach into his pocket and pull out his big steely shooter. "Huh," she thought. "He even brought it here with him."

Diane then told the story of how when she was a child her grandfather had a big jar of marbles in his workshop. She and her siblings and cousins had always tried to get their hands on those marbles and he would tell them, "keep your grubby little paws off those, they're mine."

She had loved the smell of the sawdust and varnishes that he worked with in his workshop and often sat perched on a high stool watching him work while she chattered away about nothing. Each Saturday that she was there, she would watch him close up the can of stain or varnish, wipe it with a cloth and put it away. Then he would turn off the little transistor radio and reach into the jar to pull out one single marble before he turned off the light, locked the door and held her hand as she skipped along beside him up the walkway to the house.

Once inside, he would kiss her grandmother, who was always making something delicious. Then he would go into the bedroom and close the door. Soon after, Diane would hear the clink of the marble as he dropped it into a matching jar on her grandparents' dresser. He would come out of the bedroom, wash his hands at the kitchen sink and sit down to supper.

Apparently, when he had been in his fifties, a life insurance salesman had come calling and shown him a life expectancy chart. Her grandfather was surprised to see that, according to the chart, he had so few years left. He bought the life insurance, but he also bought two jars and filled one with the same number of marbles that the chart showed he had weeks left in those remaining years.

Each Saturday, he chose a marble from the jar, reflected on how he had spent that week and thought about how he would choose to spend the next week. As he transferred each marble, one week at a time, from the jar where he worked to the one in the bedroom he shared with Diane's grandmother, he had created a visual reminder of what mattered and how to make his choices.

Diane finished the story by saying, "There were still marbles left in that jar in the workshop when he died."

The room was quiet, although she could see them each looking at their marble, or rolling it around between their fingers.

Quietly, she asked, "What choices will you make each time you reach into your pocket and feel this marble resting among the other trappings of life that call for your attention?"

The group sat quietly for a long time, listening to the popping and shifting of the logs in the fireplace. Diane noticed the young man had reached for his grandfather's hand and some of the others were exchanging looks with each other, nodding their understanding of the preciousness of this journey.

As the group broke up to head to their cabins for the night, even Jesse was glad Liza had instituted her "no device" policy. It had been a long time since he'd had such intimate conversations, and these people—could it have been only yesterday he saw them as strangers?—were becoming like friends.

⋀ Chutes and Ladders

Marty was the first one up. He couldn't wait to get out to the glacier. This was the big moment he'd been waiting for and it took all of his self-restraint to not rush everyone else out of their beds, just like when he was five and wanted to see if Santa had brought him that new red bike. He remembered, suddenly, that he hadn't gotten what he'd hoped for then and was flooded with worry that he would be disappointed today. What if it wasn't as grand as he thought it would be?

He decided to distract himself by making the coffee. He started the fire to warm the chalet and had already downed three cups of coffee by the time Liza came in, eyes bright with delight, her cheeks pink from the cold wind that was making the windows rattle, so he was a little more wired than usual.

"It's today," she said to Marty.

"I can't wait!" he cried out, his voice louder than he had intended. "Sorry, I'm just so excited, I could hardly sleep last night."

"That's good, because you're going to experience something today that will be even more thrilling than you expect."

"I hope so. I was just sitting here hoping I hadn't built it up too much in my mind and that I'd be disappointed."

"You won't be," said Liza, stirring honey into her tea. "Wanna help me get breakfast started?"

"Anything to keep me occupied and stop me from rousting the sleepyheads from their beds so we can get going already," said Marty. "I really can't wait."

"I know. Just a little longer, Marty." She said, smiling in that way that made her nose crinkle. "Let's get started on the breakfast."

Over the next hour, the chalet filled with the other travelers who had spent the night, some annoyingly bright and chipper and others clearly grumbly until they'd had their requisite java, remarking how cold it had become overnight. Marius said it would warm up a little over the next few hours but that a cold front was moving in. They might see snow tonight.

There's a storm coming!

Weather was the main topic over a breakfast of heaping plates of scrambled eggs and French toast. Marty had no idea powdered eggs could taste so good and he'd enjoyed helping Liza in the kitchen. It had occupied his hands and his mind. Marjorie never let him help at home; she was protective of her "office," as she called it.

"Liza, keep an eye on the weather and make sure you take the radio with you today, OK?" said Marius. They had both been up here in some pretty rough storms and knew it would take their combined wits to make sure their guests were safe out on the glacier. "If I hear it's changing up there or you spot anything that looks off, get off the glacier and get back here." His tone was calm but Diane noticed that his eyes were fierce as he spoke. "Even if it means cutting things short or not getting out on the ice. The glacier is not a place to take chances."

Liza nodded her understanding and Marty was suddenly looking anxious. "What? Wait a minute—we might not get to walk on the glacier today?" His voice was halfway between a sob and a shout. Everyone else looked up and conversation stopped.

"What's going on?" "What's happening?" said several people at once.

"There's a storm coming in," Marius explained. "It's not predicted to hit until tonight or tomorrow, but things are unpredictable here. The likelihood is that you're going to be fine and you'll get to spend an hour or two out there on the Lady, but you've got to keep your wits about you and know that staying safe is more important than anything. Liza knows what she's doing, she'll have the radio and we'll be in touch while you're out there."

Marty's face had fallen and some of the others' anxieties were rising. Some were worried about falling, dangers they had understandably minimized in agreeing to come on this trip, and others were worried about getting snowed in and not getting home on time—they had put things on hold to come on this trip.

One step at a time. We've got a plan.

"Alright, everybody breathe," said Liza. "We're going to take it one step at a time. We've got a plan," she said, nodding toward Marius, "and we're going to keep an eye on things out there from both ends so we can do both: give Marty and the rest of you the experience of a lifetime, just like we've planned, *and* keep everyone safe. We can do both, but it means being willing to adjust as we go and not get caught up in forcing an agenda. We'll be agile, we'll stay tuned into what's going on around us and we'll slow down or take a step back and regroup if we need to.

"But, for now, fill your bellies because you'll be surprised how much energy you'll burn on this part of the trip. It's a short trail, but it's steep, and being on crampons with ice poles out on the glacier will challenge your balance," she added.

"But," added Marius, "it'll be worth every single step. Prepare to be stunned by what you're going to experience."

The dining room was filled with a mix of excited and nervous chatter, silverware clanking against dishes and offers to each other of the final morsels left on the serving plates.

Underneath the excitement, though, people were assessing their choices and using all the ways they knew to balance the fear of missing out against the risk of getting what they wanted. Marty and Jim were clearly the ones most anxious to get out on the glacier and not miss the narrowing window of time, and they were subtly pushing the others to not dilly-dally. In fact, their sighs of impatience were audible when they realized the tables needed to be cleared and the dishes done before they could leave.

Liza and Diane could barely contain their smirks when Jesse volunteered to help Marty and Jim clean up so the others could go get ready. And with that urging, as the men began pulling plates out from in front of others who were still eating, the final swigs of coffee went down and the group disbursed to get their gear for the trek to the glacier.

As Liza was giving instructions about how to fasten the crampons on their boots when they got to the glacier edge, the young man and his grandparents appeared, their gear in tow.

Liza said, "You know you can leave your backpacks here at the chalet and pick them up when you come off the glacier. That's a lot of extra weight to carry out and back when you don't have to."

"Actually," said the young man, "we've decided to skip it and head down the trail. We don't want to risk getting caught in the storm."

"Really? You're not going to even go another mile and a half? Just to see it?" asked Marty, dumbfounded that anyone would come all this way and decide not to go the next little way, at least to see what they were walking away from.

"We're tired and just want to get back down to the lodge and have a shower and a good meal, and sleep in a comfy bed," said the grandmother. "And we don't have the kind of gear you brought, so we'd only get to go to the edge anyway, and what good is that?" Liza explained that, although she was taking her group farther out on the glacier, they would still be able to walk out a little on the glacier on their own with just their hiking boots and still have an amazing experience and feel the reward of their journey.

The trio would have none of it; they were turning back. "But, you guys enjoy it," the grandfather said. They waved as they headed down the trail away from the chalet toward the main road.

Jim was shaking his head in disbelief as he watched the departing hikers' backs. He said under his breath to Rob, "They're like the sellers who hit a bump in the process and decide it's too hard and pull out."

"Yeah," said Rob, "it's easy to underestimate the stamina it takes to be willing to go the distance. But still, to be this close and drop out. I never understand it and it always makes me shake my head. I've tried over and over to keep discouraged sellers in a deal and I always feel like I'm the one dragging them to the end. It's exhausting."

Diane overheard the conversation and added, "That's why we hired Liza to guide us through this trip. Could we have done it without her? Sure, but look how she was able to look ahead and see the things we couldn't anticipate and organize things we probably couldn't have, like having the supplies and gear brought up for us, instead of hauling it all on our backs. I'm guessing she had a reason for every one of those rest stops we made along the trail, too. Her guidance is probably why we stayed two nights here instead of just one, like those hikers planned to do. It would have been easy to feel overwhelmed with the prospect of heading all the way out to the glacier and back and then down the Highline Trail to the road and on to the lodge. I'm guessing a lot of less experienced hikers without a guide do what they did—go part way and then cut out. Or they try to make it all the way out and back and then arrive at the road utterly worn down or injured.

"Liza also helped to keep everyone moving yesterday and was able to inject the right amount of motivation when one of our guys was dragging or was trying to push the others to keep up at a pace that was untenable. Could any of us have done that for all of the others?" she asked.

"Yeah, you're right, at times it was all I could do to just carry my own weight and keep my eyes on the trail," said Rob.

"To be honest," added Jim, "Jesse and I were so impatient, we would have just powered on through and left everyone else behind, which would have kind of sucked, wouldn't it? Not much of a team experience then, I guess."

Diane gave them a moment to think and then said, "There's a parallel here for what happens in a deal, guys. As professionals, we all know that every deal has rough spots. How does the saying go? 'Every deal dies seven deaths?'" Jim and Rob nodded.

"But our sellers don't know that. Just like those hikers don't seem to know that no matter what a guidebook says, the trail is sometimes slippery and it helps to have a guide. Remember the children's game Chutes and Ladders, or Snakes and Ladders?" Both men kind of shrugged, pulling up a vague memory.

"Players are elated when they hit a ladder, imagining a swift victory as they approach the goal. But, inevitably, a later spin lands them on a chute that drops them back lower on the board. Sometimes the chutes and ladders are long, sometimes short. Each time, up or down, the player's emotions move high or low. And sometimes they miss the chutes and the ladders and just move their piece one square at a time, avoiding the obstacles, slow and steady," she said.

We know where the ladders and chutes are

"It's like that in the sale of a business, right? Except that in the game, all the players can see the end goal and they can all see exactly how much farther they have to go. In a sale, *we* can see the whole board," she indicated the whole group, "*we* know where the ladders and chutes are. Since we've played the game a lot, we're not rocked by the ups and downs—unlike our clients.

"And sometimes, like those hikers who decided it's not worth the continued ups and downs, a player gets frustrated and sweeps the pieces off the board and leaves. For them, the goal at the end, landing on the winner's circle, isn't their goal. We heard it just now. Seeing the glacier wasn't their goal. No matter how much Marty or Liza told them about what they would see, or what they would be giving up by walking away, it wasn't their 'jackpot.'"

"Kind of like when a seller is in the process because their spouse wants them to sell, but it's not really what they want."

Jim rubbed his chin, thinking. "What do you think might have been their jackpot?" he asked.

"I don't know, but if I was going to guess, maybe they convinced themselves they'd try it again some other time," Diane guessed.

"The 'next year' thing!" said Rob.

"Or maybe they were worried they'd be disappointed," said Jim. "Marty told me at one point that he was so focused on building the business all those years that he thought it might feel like a letdown when he sold it."

"We won't know because we're not in their heads," said Diane.

"Why didn't you ask them? You're good at figuring it out," asked Rob. "Don't you feel bad that they're missing out on something so amazing after they'd already put in so much effort to get here? You might have been able to change their minds and they could have come along with us, at least to see the danged thing."

"I do feel bad, Rob. But I've learned that there is huge a difference between a willing client and one who is committed to resisting at all costs. They might have been either, but it would have taken some time to figure it out. Besides, I'm here with you guys to mark something amazing with our boy Marty, not to get involved in other people's situations."

She nodded toward the others, "Speaking of, looks like Liza's ready for us to make our move." They slung their day packs on, careful to avoid hitting each other with the crampons laced to their packs, picked up their ice poles and were off, bringing up the rear, aware that Marty was radiating enthusiasm at the head of the pack.

⋀ Uncertainty Takes a Toll

They moved along the trail from the chalet toward the glacier, following the sparsely placed rock cairns. Andrew asked whether the cairns had to be rebuilt every year. Liza said yes, because heavy snow blanketed this area each year, in some years reaching the roof of the chalet, so the cairns usually fell apart. His eyes were wide. Even in Buffalo, where he had grown up, that kind of snowfall was rare nowadays.

The trail maneuvered around boulders the size of refrigerators, along mossy paths and among smaller rocks. Occasionally, they posed for pictures. They paused in silence when they came upon a group of mountain goats nibbling the lichen on the rocks.

The path narrowed and they were now walking single file. Although they had been hiking steadily for a while and the incline was moderate, the excitement was carrying everyone at a good pace. Diane realized her cheeks felt colder than they had when the group had left the chalet and she wondered if it was because they were getting close to the glacier. "How close are we, Liza?"

"It should be around this rock fall," she answered.

"'Should be'?" asked Jesse. "You don't know?"

Liza paused the group, "No, we never know for sure, Jesse. Each year, the glaciers have been retreating further and further as they continue to melt. Remember the pictures we saw at the visitors' center? The ones that showed the glaciers over the past hundred years since the national park was formed? The chalet was built where it was because back then, in 1914, it actually overlooked the glacier."

"Oh my God, it's retreated that far already?" said Andrew.

"Yeah," said Liza. "It's why that group that turned back, thinking they can come again some other time, will be stunned to find that, even if they make the time to come, and have the physical health to make the climb again, one day—we don't know how soon—the glaciers won't be here to see anymore. Or at least they will be so diminished that visitors will be disappointed, thinking they were going to find something massive but it has actually melted away to nothing reminiscent of what it was, or even is today."

"Idiots" whispered someone.

"Not idiots," said Diane gently, "just people who are unsure and aren't able to see around what stands in their way. Without Liza, I might not be willing to venture out onto the ice either. We're lucky to have you with us." She nodded to her friend with a smile.

"Truly, it's my honor to accompany you on this part of the journey. And this is one reason this trip that Marty has created is so very special for all of you. You are going to see something you'll probably never see again and that only a fraction of the visitors to this park are brave enough to try."

Only a fraction are brave enough to try

Marty beamed with pride, happy that he was going to share something so magical with the people who had helped him climb his own mountain in selling his company.

"So let's go already!" he said, no longer able to contain his excitement. He was about to walk on a glacier!

As they came around the rock fall, they stopped, surprised to see only the gravel, boulders and scree of the moraine. No glacier in sight. Marty's disappointment was palpable. Liza tapped his shoulder, "Look at me, Marty. It's just further than we originally thought. Don't worry, we're going to get there."

"But you said …" his voice trailed off. He hated that he sounded like a child.

"I know, just keep following the cairns; it's out there," she said.

"Maybe we took the wrong trail," said Jesse, a hint of irritation in his voice. "Are you sure this is the way?"

We always want to be on the right path

Andrew asked, "Do we still have enough time? Should we check the weather? We don't want to get caught in the storm."

Liza took a deep breath and turned to face the group. "OK, hold on." Addressing Jesse she said, "Your question makes sense, Jesse—we always want to make sure we're on the right path; that's why we've been following the cairns; they mark the way of guides who have gone ahead of us. We can tell we're on track by looking out ahead and spotting the way they're leading—do you see them?" she asked, pointing across the moraine they were about to tackle. "See the one there on top of that squarish boulder? And that one further on, along the cliff wall about eight feet high?"

"Yeah, OK. Sorry, I guess you're right," he said.

"Never apologize for stopping to ask. No one is certain all the time and it helps to be able to pause and look around, and change course if we need to," she responded. "Andrew, you're right to wonder, too. I'll radio Marius. He has insight we may not have." She reached into her pack and pulled out the radio. She described where they were. Marius said all indications were that they'd have another three hours of decent weather and that the last guide to return had said they'd have another mile or so to the edge of the glacier, another thirty to forty minutes if they were able to keep a good pace. Marty's face fell, "But that means we won't have much time at the glacier if we have to cover this same distance to get back before the storm."

Dan stepped in and said, "Marty, don't get caught up in worry. Let's keep going and evaluate things when we get to it. We'll see what the conditions are. Things can change, and we're adaptable, buddy."

"OK, watch your footing, everyone," Liza said. "It's rocky, and while we're making good time, safety comes first." She turned, adding, "Don't worry Marty, we're almost there. You heard it, right?" And they resumed their single file trek in search of their mighty frozen goal.

They hadn't been able to see the glacier because although it had retreated, the edge of the glacier was there just around that right cliff wall where the high cairn had been.

Shouts of "Whoa!" and "Holy shit!" erupted from the group, but mostly there were slack jaws when they saw the vast sheet of ice before them.

"It's so much bigger than I thought!" said Andrew. Marty's eyes were fixed straight ahead, fascinated by the multi-hued ice sheet splayed out across the terrain. He was surprised that it was blue and gray and white and black and shades he couldn't quite capture in his mind.

"I thought it would be melting into a river or something," said Jesse.

"It is," said Liza, "but the flow is in that direction," she pointed. "Much of the water flow happens under the surface, although some of it is on top, too, this late in the season. While we can walk some distance out in just our boots, let's get our crampons on here, at the edge where you can feel secure, and then we'll venture out a bit and see where to go." She helped them get the spiky ice grips securely fastened to their boots and took some photos of them at the edge where rock became ice. Then she pointed out the small cairns that were out on the glacier, indicating paths that prior guides had marked as safe.

"But I thought we'd get to go where no one else had gone," said Marty. He realized he sounded like he was in a Star Trek movie with that last remark and made the Vulcan salute like Mr. Spock, which made the others laugh.

"There are lots of different paths for us to follow, Marty," said Liza. "We're going to stay where it's safe, though, OK? We're adven-tourists, not Lewis and Clark, right? We've talked about this: there are ice holes and dangerous areas, and this trip is about a bigger experience. You won't be disappointed, I promise." Diane noticed that Jesse was hanging back from the group, rolling the marble between his ungloved fingers and staring up at the sky. She nodded to Liza to take the group ahead. She'd follow with Jesse in a minute.

As the group stepped onto the edge of the glacier and started to move, Diane approached Jesse, "What's happening?" she inquired gently.

"Nothing," he said reflexively.

"It's OK," she said, "we can talk, or we can just stand here for a minute; your choice." She was used to creating companionable silence while her clients sorted through their thoughts and feelings, deciding what to share.

Minutes ticked by, both of them watching the figures of the others shrinking in size compared to the mass of the glacier they were walking upon. Finally, Jesse said, "I have … I'm sick." They were both still looking straight ahead, not making eye contact.

Diane thought for a moment. "Like your grandmother?" The barely perceptible drop of his head told her she was correct. "Do you want to talk about it?" she asked quietly.

"Not really. There's not much to say." He shrugged. "They think it's spread pretty far already." He sounded resigned.

"Does your wife know?" she asked, still affording him some privacy by not making eye contact.

"Not yet. But I'm not going to be able to keep it from her much longer," he allowed himself to let out the sob that had been building for weeks. "We're not ready, we haven't paid off the house yet and the business … Our kids are …" his voice trailed off.

She asked, "Can I just hold your hand while we talk?" He shrugged, but let her take his hand as they continued to stand side by side, small together in a vast and unpredictable space.

"This is a lot for you to hold all by yourself, Jesse. How long have you known?"

"I've suspected something was wrong for a while. But I've been so damned busy and it was easier to just put off getting it checked. Honestly, I just thought it was hemorrhoids or something. You know, when I'm busy I don't always eat the best," he said. "They told me two weeks ago. I'm supposed to see the oncologist next week. He wanted to see me right away but I figured I've got to get this deal wrapped up first, if I'm gonna do it, especially if it's as bad as they think." He squeezed her hand, stammering, "I … I don't think … I might not be able to work pretty soon."

She squeezed his hand back, nodding, but not offering any shallow platitudes or hollow reassurances that everything would be OK when they both knew it might not. Yes, she helped her clients see the best in situations, but not as a way to squelch their fears. Plenty of people would offer him the "look on the bright side" denials. For now, she just stood with him, on the brink of starkly different landscapes, holding this uncertainty with him. "What do you need?" she asked.

"A fucking miracle," he answered, dropping her hand and stepping onto the edge of the ice sheet. He put on his glove and stabbed the ice pole into the glacier. "Let's get out there and see what Marty's big dream is all about," he said, pushing down the conversation they'd just had. Diane took a breath and followed him, silently grateful that Karen had chosen to be with her father-in-law and that this man was here among courageous others she was certain would support him if she could help him find a way to let them in. The contrast of Jesse's understandably darkened mood against the oddly pale blue sky created a starkness she wasn't sure how to name.

They made their way out across the ice, following the footprints of the others to the little semi-circle they had formed. Liza was pointing out the features of the glacier. As they arrived, Marty turned and said, "Jesse, come here," motioning him to take a spot between him and Dan. Jesse stepped into the spot the two men created for him. Marty said, "I've never felt so damn small as I do looking out at this," he said waving his hand at the ice that went on for miles behind and beyond them.

"Yeah," said Jesse.

Liza motioned for them to turn and face west. From that angle they were looking down the glacier to where it dipped between the mountains, eventually melting into the glacial river that fed Lake McDonald. She handed the binoculars to Marty first and pointed for him to look in that direction, "That's Lake McDonald Lodge, where we'll be staying tomorrow night." The others strained their eyes to look where Liza was pointing until it was their turn to look through the binoculars.

"Today you stand near the head of the glacier and tomorrow night you'll sleep near its foot. The meltwater makes its journey more directly down the slope; our path will be less direct. We're going to go back down the Highline Trail," she said pointing back toward where the chalet was. "Then we'll pick up the hiker shuttle, follow Going-to-the-Sun Road along the back side of this mountain here," **Same end point, different ways to get there.** she said pointing, "and come out down there" gesturing to the lodge at the base of the lake. "Same end point, different ways to get there.

"Lots of travelers will have seen that part of the journey along the road. That part actually has more than three million visitors a year, but few see this—the bigger view of how vast this land is and how rough the terrain is. But you have, Marty, you have," she smiled at the one whose vision they were sharing.

His face was bright with delight. He shook his head and whispered, emotion preventing him from giving full voice. "It's even bigger and more spectacular than I imagined."

The group was quiet, each taking in the scene before them from their unique vantage point, trying to understand how they fit into the vastness of the world that surrounded them, so much of it hidden from everyone but those who were willing to journey.

Diane and Liza smiled at each other, knowing they had brought something to this group, a shared experience that would connect them in ways that reached beyond their professional relationships with each other, something profound and enduring.

"Liza, are you still on the glacier?" the radio hanging from her waist crackled.

"Yeah, I'm here," she answered. "But we're about to head back." She heard the group's murmured protests and knew they would have loved to stay longer. "What's up?"

The voice across the radio said, "Storm's coming in off the backside. Looks like it'll crest the ridge in forty, sixty tops."

"Ok, thanks, we're heading in. I'll let you know when we're off the ice."

"Roger that."

"You guys heard it. Two last pictures, OK? One looking down toward the lake. Good. Now, one up the glacier," she said, walking around the group to snap the second photo, their backs to the ridge. Although she said "Smile!" she saw what the radio had warned: the sky was darkening and she knew it was time to get them off the ice. At least if the storm hit and they were on the trail, they'd be wet and miserable, but not in danger.

"OK, let's go, guys. Steady; use your poles and we'll follow the footprints back the way we came. Stay close to each other. No straggling." Her tone was light. She didn't need them to be scared; that just made things worse and she couldn't afford to have anyone injured. She'd done this trip enough to spot the changing sky. The others saw only the big white clouds in an oddly dark blue sky that made for a beautiful backdrop to the dark cliff side and the brilliant glacier. It would be a gorgeous shot for them to frame as a memento of this trip. But for now, she had no time to congratulate herself on her photography skills. She had seven glacier rookies to get back safely.

Although Liza hadn't drawn their attention to it, everyone had heard the words "forty, sixty tops," and although they didn't know exactly how long they had been on the ice because they had been taking in the awe of it all, they all knew it had taken them longer than sixty minutes to make it from the chalet to the edge of the glacier. Each of them was trying to keep themselves calm, hoping that no one else was also thinking, "this is bad."

They made it off the ice and as they were detaching their crampons, Liza said, "OK, we're off the ice. That's crucial. But you all know we're about to face a storm, right?" They nodded, some with eyes wider than others. "Secure the crampons to your day packs like this so the spikes aren't facing out. We may get hit with some wind and you don't need those razor sharp things crashing into people or into you if you stumble. Keep the poles, they'll be good to help you balance as we make our way down the trail to the chalet. She radioed in that they were off the ice and headed across the moraine.

"It's important that we stay together, so no one jump ahead. We don't want to miss any of the cairns or have anyone get lost. We'll move as quickly as we can, but stay alert and, remember, safety continues to be our mantra, right?" Andrew and Jim offered to bring up the rear. They knew that if they had to, they could help if anyone fell or turned an ankle among the rocks and gravel.

They headed back the way they came, across the moraine, with a new appreciation for the fact that all of this once lay beneath the surface of the great glacier. As they crossed the last of it and were back on the actual trail, Liza stopped them and said, "Look back at what you've just crossed. Remember when we were here earlier and weren't able to yet see what we were headed for? Now that you've stood on the glacier, see how far it stretched? See what used to be beneath it, and what it's left in the wake of its retreat? Can you feel the greatness and the power of it?

"I want you to be able to take in the resilience, the strength of what you've done so far. To feel what's on the other side of the disappointment you felt when we were here earlier and we wondered whether we had gone the wrong way, not knowing how much farther we had to go and whether it was even there, and not really knowing what we would see when we got there."

She was trying to inspire them and help them to lock in the wonder of it all before they faced the next challenge. "You did this today. Together."

They smiled and looked into each other's faces with a sense of pride. They had done something amazing together.

"We're back on the trail here, but keep watching for the cairns and stay together. Keep your eyes on the path and watch your step. You already know there are lots of rocks as we head down and that moss and lichen will get slippery if the rain gets to us before we get to the chalet." They all looked up, trying to read the sky as it was changing above them, but they didn't know what it meant. "We'll make better time than we did coming up because we're going down. But keep an eye on each other. This isn't a time to show how macho you are. Slow and steady and we all get there safe."

She radioed in with their location, and the voice responded, "It seems to have stalled over Mount Gould. You've got more time than we thought, but don't dawdle, keep 'em moving."

"Right-o," she said, and the group began moving down the trail again.

Diane was sorry they hadn't had more time to focus on the celebratory aspect of their feat when they were on the ice or to allow for the slow unwinding of the experience among them, as she had hoped would happen with a more leisurely return to the chalet, but then again, she knew they would each be processing it as they hiked.

Nearly an hour later, the group stomped into the chalet and started dropping packs and outerwear onto chairs and the floor. Marius already had the fire going, which helped to take the chill off their damp clothes and bodies. Liza was gathering the poles and crampons and packing them back into a bin to be picked up when the supply helicopter came to the chalet next week, likely for the last time that season.

Diane emerged from the kitchen with the coffee pot and said, "Grab a mug if you want some java, fellas." She had brought out the leftover cornbread muffins and a tin of butter cookies Liza had shipped up. In short order, the treats were gone and the group was excitedly talking over each other, sharing their perceptions of the grandeur they had witnessed. Their amygdalas had calmed down and the other memories were surfacing and being shared.

"Come sit for a bit, Liza." Diane motioned her to join them at the long table. "I'll help you pack that up before we start dinner. Just let yourself unwind, girl; that was intense."

Several of them started to yawn. Marty asked what time dinner would be and whether they had time for a little nap. Liza said that while she'd planned an early supper for that night, they easily had time for a snooze. The group broke up and some headed to their cabins. Others nodded off in the big chairs by the fire.

⩕ Listening for a Legacy

The steaming bowls of pasta disappeared quickly, filling bellies and fueling bodies for the cold night ahead.

The kitchen was still warm from the oven as Diane and Jesse finished drying the dishes. He knew she wanted to continue the conversation they had begun on the edge of the glacier and, while he knew he could avoid her and she wouldn't chase him down on it, he also felt some relief in having someone else know his burden.

She had washed the dishes, wearing that ridiculous floral apron, handing him plate after bowl to dry and stack on the counter to be put away. She picked up a dry dish towel and turned to face him as they dried forks and spoons. He thought it was odd, their silence. He didn't think he'd ever met a woman who didn't have to always be talking, and it had given him space to think as they did the dishes. He thought maybe this is what it means to "hold space." He'd heard the phrase, but until now, he hadn't had any idea what it meant and how helpful it could be.

"Are you open to a suggestion?" she asked.

"I guess."

"May I help you to share this with the others tonight?" she ventured softly.

"The others? You mean Marty and the rest?" he sounded panicked. "What for?"

"What do you think it would be for, Jesse?" she set down three dry forks and picked up several spoons, polishing them long after they were dry while she waited for him to answer.

"I don't know. I guess … I do feel better now that you know, so I guess for more of that. But won't that make it even less likely that Dan will want to buy my company?" His words began tumbling out. "I mean, who wants to buy a company whose founder is gonna croak at any moment?" His fear was escalating and he was talking faster and faster. "Won't that just give them a way to pay rock bottom or just wait and steal it out from under me when I'm too sick to fight them? I mean, my family is gonna need this money …"

Diane put her hand on his arm and said gently, "Jesse, take a breath." She waited. "Can you feel it? How fear just got the better of you?"

They stood in the kitchen, with the murmur of voices in the other room sometimes punctuated by laughter, just breathing together.

When he had calmed himself he said, "That's a mighty crazy lizard." His crooked smile told her that his brain had come back on line and she could continue.

"It is, and it makes sense that you would feel hypervigilant and fall into that pattern of wariness, and pull away." Jesse nodded briefly.

"Do you think, with this part," she asked, tapping her forehead, "that Dan would try to steal your business and screw you? Or is that fear talking?"

"I don't know. I don't think he would, but …" his voice trailed off.

"Jesse, I don't have a dog in this hunt. I have no incentive to make you trust Dan. But I do know that you came on this trip for a reason. What do you think it was?"

"'Cause Dan and Marty asked me."

She was silent but her eyes said, "Bullshit" and he knew it.

"I came because … I guess because I'm scared. And I need to figure out how I'm going to save my company while I fight like hell for my life." She stood quietly, waiting for more.

"And," he admitted with a shrug, "I wanted to figure out if these guys were for real and whether I could trust them."

"So, how will you know?" she asked.

He let out a long sigh, "I guess I've gotta tell them."

"No, Jesse, there's nothing you've gotta do. It's yours to tell and I won't breach your confidence. But I do think you will learn a lot. About yourself and about those men, if you decide to. And I will help you if you want me to."

She turned to fill the kettle and soon felt the cold blow against her back. Jesse had walked out into the rising snow. Diane wiped her hands on the apron, knowing he would take the space he needed and she'd simply wait.

This was another night that ended with the embers burning down, but this time, they sat silently, each lost in their own thoughts about what they had seen and heard today.

Liza broke the silence. "I think the snow has stopped." They all turned their eyes to the darkened windows. She was glad she had suggested they bring their sleeping bags into the chalet; the cabins weren't heated. Liza was uncertain whether the snow would continue overnight and told them it was their choice whether they wanted to return to their cabins to sleep or to lay their sleeping bags on the floor around the living room and stay warmer by the fire. It was funny that this group, who made big decisions every day, deferred to what she thought they should do.

"It's really your choice," she answered. "We'll see how things look in the morning after breakfast. In the light, the rangers will be able to tell us how the roads are and what conditions we might face on the trail."

Marty turned to Jesse and said, "What would you like, Jesse?" The others looked to him, too, oddly comfortable with the experience of offering their support in the face of what he had shared with them over the past hour.

Jesse looked surprised when he lifted his gaze and saw the others smiling toward him. He hadn't ever been part of a group of men who weren't trying to beat each other out. He'd been on sports teams where there'd been a kind of camaraderie among teammates, but this felt different, warmer. He swallowed and looked to Diane. She nodded and raised her eyebrow, encouraging him to say what he truly wanted.

Vulnerability leads to closeness

"I dunno. You guys can do what's right for you." He was still reeling from the vulnerability it had taken to share his cancer diagnosis with the others. Although Diane had suspected how it would go, she had still been in awe of how the group had embraced him, literally and figuratively, and how they had then each shared their own struggles and strengths.

"Jesse," Diane asked. "Would it feel better for you to be surrounded by people who care about you?"

He lowered his gaze, unable to say how very much he wanted that. Sadly, because he was looking down, he also missed seeing how much each of them also wanted that closeness. Vulnerability opened the way for closeness, but it was still difficult for them to ask for what they needed.

Marty was watching Jesse carefully. "Get ready to live through Dan's polar bear snoring, buddy-boy!" said Marty. Andrew protested, "Look who's talking! You're like a moose! We could hear you both through the wall last night." And with that the men started moving the chairs and couches out of the way. Diane rescued coffee cups from tables and moved them to the kitchen sink as more logs were added to the fire and the floor of the lodge became a bivouac, sleeping bags dropped everywhere. Through the kitchen window, Diane said a silent thank you to the stars that had begun to show their faces in the frigid night sky.

They lay in the dark, listening to the sounds of the fire for a long time, each suspecting that what had passed in this lodge tonight would ripple into their lives in ways none of them could know. Only Dan saw the moment when night slipped into day, as he lay awake, listening to the slumbering sounds of the others, outlining a plan.

The groans and throat clearing coughs of older men, awaking from a night spent sleeping on the floor, was the telling sign that morning had arrived. And it wasn't just the older guys who silently questioned what the hell they were thinking when they had agreed to sleep on the floor.

"I'm too damned old for this," murmured Rob as his throbbing knee reminded him of the tumble he'd taken yesterday making his way back from the glacier. He winced at the thought of today's downhill hike, through snow, no less. His dreams had been filled with that massive glacier, and he was still trying to shake the thought of how he had been unable to grasp Jesse's hand as he fell into a deep crevasse in his dream. Rob was still unsettled by the sound of Jesse's screams in the dream as he rolled his sleeping bag and tied the strings around it tightly.

"Good morning!" crowed Diane, as she brought cups to the table, along with the fragrant coffee pot.

"That woman is insane," thought Jim, who never spoke to anyone until he'd had at least three cups of coffee. He was glad his wife had learned that lesson early in their years together. Every assistant he'd had learned it quickly, too.

Diane nodded for Jesse to follow her into the kitchen. He stretched his arms above his head, wondering what she was going to ask him to do next.

"How are you feeling?" she asked.

"Stiff and sore like everyone else."

"No, I meant about sharing last night with the group."

"You know, I'm not sure. I was worried that this morning I'd regret it or feel, I don't know, like … an emotional hangover." He scratched his belly. "But, I actually feel relieved." She nodded. "I'd built it up in my mind that they would screw me. I guess last night made me realize that I hadn't ever really, you know, let anyone get close to me since I started the business."

"That makes sense," she said. "A lot of founders feel isolated, like they have to carry every problem on their own and, like you, they can feel a tremendous—but unfamiliar—sense of relief when they get to show their real selves, especially to other men," she added. "The odd part is that although most of us worry that showing vulnerability will make us seem weak, typically it creates closer connections and leads to a sense of respect from the people you let in. Don't be surprised, though, if you do feel that sense of fear coming back, making you second guess whether you did the right thing in sharing. It's normal. Just stay with it and observe what happens when you bring trustworthy people around you. And don't get sidetracked by other people who tell you you were nuts and try to scare you into guarding around these good people who have your back."

> Note what happens with trustworthy people around you

"That helps, Diane, really. Because I've already had those thoughts this morning, lying on my back feeling fully exposed."

She nodded, "I know."

The sound of tables and chairs and sofas being shoved into place brought them back to the moment, and Jesse was out the kitchen door again with a whoosh of cold air.

Gathering a handful of spoons and the bowls for oatmeal, Diane looked out the window and smiled. She nudged Liza, who was turning one more vat of powdered eggs into fluffy, scrambled goodness. "Look." She nodded with her chin toward the window.

Liza turned in time to see Marty and Jesse lifting the middle section of what looked to be a giant snowman. She realized they had no idea that Jim and Andrew were about to pound them with snowballs. The women smiled at each other and finished laying the table with food, content to let the guys have their morning of snowy fun. They had time this morning for wet clothes to dry by the fire before they made their trek back down the trail.

Soon, mouths were filled with Liza's breakfast treats. Business executives in their long johns, completely unselfconscious, ate while their snow-caked clothes and boots lay strewn around the room. Although no one spoke of it, everyone wondered who would first broach the topic hanging in the air.

Since no one else did, Jesse decided to tackle it. "I just want to say … that I really appreciate all of you guys for, well, you know, the way you handled what I had to say last night. It means a lot. And, well, I don't know what's going to happen once I get back and all, but … ah, anyway … thanks."

"You got this, man" and "We're with you" and other words of encouragement came from each of them, in between the bites of food they continued to shovel into their mouths. Only Dan was silent. He was nodding along, but Diane wondered what was happening for him and hoped Jesse wasn't also picking up on it and turning it into worry. She made a mental note to try to get some private time with Dan, just to take his emotional temperature.

Soon enough, the conversation turned to their thoughts about the glacier, the weather, the trail they would soon face and who had scored the most hits in the snowball fight this morning. Heating the water on the stove to do the last round of the dishes, Diane looked out the window and saw that the snowman was wearing her apron.

⋀ There's More Than Meets the Eye

Even though it was the last, and technically the easiest, leg of the journey, Liza wanted everyone to know that they couldn't take anything for granted as they made today's trek, especially since the first part of it would be in snow that might be knee deep in places. Though they had traversed up part of the same trail two days before, Liza reminded them that they had been able to see the terrain then. Today, their footing would be less secure and they wouldn't be able to easily tell whether tree roots or rocks lay beneath the snow.

The park rangers had told Marius that the trail was clear, just muddy for most of the way below the Garden Wall Trail intersection, and Liza decided to tell them this morning that they wouldn't face up-trail hikers because the glacier was being closed off for the rest of the season.

"Why?" several of them asked in unison.

"There's been some unusual activity on the glacier and they're investigating what might be causing it and what its impact could be."

"When did this happen?" asked Andrew. "Were we in danger yesterday?"

"Was that why you were rushing us off the glacier?" The questions came rapidly from several of them at once.

Marius jumped in. He didn't like seeing Liza under attack. "Listen guys." He raised his hand for them to pause because he could tell they were angry and scared. "Yes, we did know some of this. Liza and I talked with the rangers and the geology team ahead of time and they let us know what *would* be safe for you to do yesterday. We mapped it out together and Liza is an experienced guide. She told me what you had come up here for and we wanted to make sure that you got at least some of what you came for."

> I like to have all the facts when I make decisions

"That's all well and good and I'm enjoying your little kumbaya moment and everything," said Rob, "but I'm with Andrew. I don't like the thought that you guys had information that we didn't. I like to know what I'm dealing with and be able to make decisions with all the facts."

Jim and Jesse were nodding their agreement too, and Diane thought, "OK, here we go." Taking a breath she said, "That's a good topic, you guys. Rob," she said, turning to him, "ever hold back information from opposing counsel?"

"That's different," he protested.

"Is it? How about you, Jim? Ever been in a deal where you felt you couldn't trust the other side?"

"Of course!"

Out of the corner of her eye, she saw Liza about to protest that she was trustworthy. Diane held up her index finger briefly to signal Liza to wait. "It's the same thing as here."

"Do we have to do this again?" asked Jesse with a sigh of exasperation. "I'm really not up for another of your 'lessons' right now. I'd rather get on the trail and make some headway." Others nodded, anxious to be moving, and, she thought, anxious not to look at something we all do and at our motivations for it.

"We never *have* to do anything, Jesse," Diane reminded him. "We can always choose to skip something we can learn from. But I'm going to ask for a couple minutes of indulgence from the group because I think this *is* relevant, right now. And I think it's going to be useful for the next part of our trip together." A couple of them sighed, plopping into chairs. She ignored their petulance. Even without seeing their rolling eyes, she knew they'd learn something, despite themselves. "This is what I mean when I say we pause the content so we can deal with the context.

"For those of you who haven't heard me say that, it means this: sometimes we're so focused on addressing the content," she picked up a guide book from the table and held it parallel to the floor, "that we completely ignore the undercurrents, the context." She moved her other hand like a wave under the book.

"Ever been in a conversation with someone where you knew they just weren't getting it and you just said it louder or kept repeating the same thing, over and over?" Most of them nodded. "That's what's going on. Until the context is addressed, the content goes nowhere. We saw that just play out here. When Liza told you we wouldn't see up-trail hikers because the glacier was closed, several of you had a reaction. What was it?" she asked, looking around the room.

"Geez. Do we have to go over this every time?" Diane ignored Rob's comment.

"Anger, especially when I realized she *knew* and didn't tell us," said Andrew.

"Was it anger? Or was it surprise and then fear, and anger was the way fear expressed itself?" "Well, yeah, probably," he conceded.

"And then Liza and Marius tried to explain why they made the decision they did. And what was happening for you then?" She was addressing the whole group.

"I wondered what else they were hiding," said Jim, a look coming across his face that said he had seen where this discussion might be going.

"Right," continued Diane. "Your amygdala had been tripped with the first piece of news and it kept signaling fear as it flipped into hypervigilance, scanning the environment to see what else you were missing or they were concealing." She was moving the thumb of her left hand vigorously, as if the lizard were scanning the room for danger. "That's what happens when we learn that someone has kept something from us. Even when, as in this case, it's for our benefit.

"So can we all agree that they"—she gestured toward Liza and Marius, perched on the back of the sofa, arms crossed in a defensive posture as they tried not to react to what they felt was an unjustified attack—"were not trying to harm us?" The others nodded, some half-heartedly. "And can we see how, for them, it was justified to not tell us everything? Even though, from our vantage point, some of you think you should have received the information?" More nodding. "Recall how, upon learning it, your amygdala fired into panic mode and got you worrying about what *else* you might not know? How it interprets what it thinks is a 'lie'—and I'm using that word just for this example, not because I think they lied—as danger?"

Diane gave them a moment to think and then continued. "How many of you use 'the art of omission,' thinking it's not a lie if you're just leaving out some information, especially if no one asked you the question directly, and justifying it by thinking it's in your or another's interest and there's no harm in not sharing it? How many of you, when confronted as you just confronted Liza and Marius, would stand with your arms crossed looking indignant?" Liza and Marius self-consciously uncrossed their arms and smiled sheepishly, "thinking the other person was wrong not to trust you?"

There was a lot of thinking going on, and Jim and Rob were talking over each other. "That's all well and good in this situation, Diane," said Rob, "but I have a duty to protect my client and the attorney-client privilege says I *can't* disclose everything I know."

"Yeah," Jim agreed. "I mean, sometimes I've got to keep stuff secret. This kind of business means I'd be a fool to trust every other guy in a transaction. That's just the way this game works. But yesterday could have actually put *lives* at risk."

"OK," Diane said, "what if that story you each just told is exactly that—a story—one that you tell yourself to make it OK to play hide-the-ball, conceal information, lie and generally be untrustworthy?" She could see she had hit a nerve. Almost everyone was uncomfortable and several were chomping at the bit to defend themselves.

Diane held up her hand. "Everybody pause. Take a breath. And look at what happened, right there." The room paused while everyone took a breath or two. Some people were biting their lips to avoid blurting something out and several were looking at the floor, holding in their anger. "Now everybody breathe again. Make an effort to relax your bodies, unclench your jaws—and maybe even your fists," she laughed, "and now lift your eyes and make eye contact with each other." She waited while they did so.

> The "art of omission" is just lies

"Good. Do you know what just happened?" Faces looked quizzical.

"I got mad," said Jim. "You just said I'm a liar!" He continued with angry sarcasm, "Sometimes I think maybe you just don't understand how deals get done, Diane." A couple of people nodded their agreement. A few others were uncomfortable, believing a confrontation was coming.

She smiled, saying calmly. "Jim, do you think that's true? Do you really think I don't understand how deals get done?"

He was actively trying to calm himself and she gave him the space to do it. "No," he allowed, "I know you do. But ..." She could tell he was on the brink of escalating again.

"But my saying that it's not necessary or helpful to do things the way you've learned to do them feels threatening?" she said.

"Yeah, kind of." He was opening and closing his hands slowly, while breathing.

"That makes sense, Jim. And that's your amygdala talking. Keep breathing." Then, addressing the others, "Anyone else feel like Jim?" Hands went up.

"Of course. And what's the story that goes on in your head thanks to our little friend the lizard? Something like, 'I have to hide this information or else ...' or 'I'm not a liar, liars are bad and I'm not bad.' What else?" she prompted. "I don't doubt that lots of people are concealing information, all the time, in deals and in everyday life. But I also know it's not helpful. For anyone."

"But everybody is doing it; we can't stop them!" Jesse interrupted.

"That's correct, we can't stop anyone else," Diane responded. "Think about what drove that statement you just made. Was it fear that you'll be taken advantage of? A sense that if you don't do what everyone else is doing you'll be in danger?"

She paused, then said, "Again, everybody take a breath and relax. We're covering something tough here." She noticed that, while they were definitely uncomfortable, no one was talking about rushing out onto the trail anymore. They were engaged, so she pressed on.

The more transparent you are and the less you conceal ...

"Guess what? It's not only the thought that 'everybody else is doing it' that trips your amygdala into fear. It's that when you're concealing information, you actually trip your own amygdala." She paused to let that sink in. Their faces said they were trying to grasp the thought.

"Yep, that's right. When you're concealing information from someone, for any reason, your amygdala goes into protective mode, worried that your secret will be found out, that you'll be exposed. So by hiding information, even if you think it's for a good reason, you are flipping yourself into scared mode.

"And guess what else? Others can sense your anxiety, even when you think you're cool as a cucumber around your lie—or the thing you aren't calling a lie. Unconsciously, their amygdala can sense that something's up, but it can't quite sense what. Which escalates their fear, often making them conceal information or react in all the ways we've talked about." She flipped open her left hand, fingers splayed wide. "You're both flipping your own and each other's lids unconsciously," she said, flipping up the fingers on her right hand, too. "And then the entire conversation is just lizard-to-lizard, absolutely no prefrontal cortex to be found. Is it any wonder that when we're ignoring all of this, conversations and deals run off the rails?

"Listen," she said, "I know it's counterintuitive to believe that the more transparent you are, the more congruent your actions are with your words and the less you conceal, the safer you actually are. In fact, when you aren't concealing anything, you're better able to tell when someone else *is*. When you sense that they are, or even just that something is going on that you can't quite understand, and you choose to push

... the more safety you create

pause on addressing the content, choosing instead to openly drop into the context of what's going on beneath the surface for you and the other person, it restores a sense of safety, and then you can return to the content. I know this approach takes more time, but in the end everything runs more smoothly than if you just kept pushing on the content without clearing the context that's mucking everything up."

Diane paused to let that long thought sink in. "Need an example?" Lots of nodding.

"How many of you had a sense yesterday that Liza knew something she wasn't quite talking about?" Hands shot up. Liza's face turned red. "When did you know it and what tipped you off? Jesse?"

"When we reached the spot where it seemed like Liza thought we would see the glacier and it wasn't there, I thought her answer sounded fishy."

"OK, Liza, don't get defensive," she said to her friend, "Just take it in; stay with us." She turned back to Jesse. "And where did you feel it in your body?"

Thinking, Jesse said, "Here, in my eyes, it felt like my eyes narrowed and I tipped my head like this." He demonstrated.

"Exactly. We call that 'dog ears.' Ever see a dog do that when it's trying to figure out where a sound came from or what an unknown thing is that it can't make sense of? That's a little trigger from the amygdala: 'something's not quite adding up' it's saying, sending us a little warning about what might be danger," she said.

"Now, Liza, what happened for you when we hit that spot and the glacier wasn't there where you thought we'd find it?" Diane asked.

"My stomach clenched and I thought, 'uh-oh, did I miss a cairn? Did we go the wrong way?' I started worrying that I'd taken them into a dead end or, even worse, what if it turned out to be a dangerous spot? Then I was worried I'd look like a fool or that they'd be mad," answered Liza. "Even now, it's uncomfortable to admit it and I can feel my body tensing up."

Diane noticed that some of the others had softened their expressions. "It's hard being responsible for people and needing to look like you have all the answers." Liza nodded. "So what happened when Jesse questioned why you didn't know where the glacier was?"

"In a flash, I felt ashamed and frightened and then defiant. Luckily, I was able to tame all of that and not flame it out onto him like I would have in my old corporate life." She winked at Jesse. "Instead, I answered him as best I could, trying to reassure him that I knew what I was doing." She looked away for a moment. "Even when I was worried that maybe I actually didn't."

"Did you notice Jesse narrow his eyes and cock his head like he described?" Diane asked Liza.

"I'm not sure if I noticed consciously, but I realize that I was paying extra attention to whether Jesse was going to challenge me again, especially as we got closer to the glacier, and I knew I needed to be able to control the situation more than I normally would, without scaring anyone." She looked toward Jesse and said, "Since we'd already tangled a bit about the phone, I was conscious that you could go a little rogue … or that's the story I made up in my mind," she quickly corrected.

"Jesse, did you pick up on that tension in Liza?"

"Uh-huh. Even early on I was resistant to trusting her. Sorry, Liza, I've had a pattern of challenging authority; it's not about you." She nodded an acknowledgment and he continued. "In fact, I can say that I haven't really trusted anyone. Here on the trip, or really in most parts of my life. That is, until last night, I guess."

"Thanks, Jesse, hang with that for a minute." Diane then asked, "Did anyone sense before last night that Jesse might be hiding something?" Lots of nodding, and Andrew said, "I kept trying to figure out what was causing the chip on your shoulder, Jesse. Last night, I realized some of the things that could be under it and I was lying there thinking about how scared you must be—about a lot of things: the cancer and your business and your family."

"And how did that change what you thought about Jesse's chip on the shoulder?" Diane asked.

"Actually, it made a lot more sense. And instead of wanting to knock it off his shoulder—" he turned to Jesse"—sorry man, that's just the way I was feeling before I knew what was going on." Jesse shrugged his acknowledgment. "Well, instead of being pissed at him, I realized 'oh man, that's a lot of weight he's carrying' and I was lying there trying to figure out how I could help. Maybe carry some of it with you." Jesse looked surprised. "Yeah," continued Andrew, "actually, there are some annuity things and stuff that I'd love to go over with you to take the pressure off about worrying about your family while you're going through … you know, treatment and stuff." Diane noticed it was hard for them to contain the emotion they felt for this young man who two days ago had been a stranger to most of them.

"Jesse, what is it like to hear Andrew say that?" she asked.

"I'm kind of embarrassed about being such a dick before." His head was hanging.

Diane paused him to ask, "What if you lift your head and look at Andrew when you talk to him?"

He looked away instead. "I … I don't know if …"

Rob put his hand on Jesse's back. "It's OK, man. Take your time."

Jesse took a couple of deep breaths, raised his head and said, "Thanks, Andrew. That means a lot. Really." He let out a fast breath. "I was so scared. Of all of you. Partly because my lawyer told me I shouldn't come on this trip, that it was a trick to rope me into a deal." He shrugged a little, trying to meet Dan's eyes, but Dan was leaning back against his chair, eyes closed, the steeple of his fingers under his chin, which unnerved Jesse and he rushed on, "Plus, you all seemed to know each other and I felt like a fifth wheel." Looking over at Marty, "I mean, don't think I'm not grateful, Marty, because I am. You've been so generous to me and from the beginning did everything to make me feel welcome. Even your wife hugging me at the train station. I can't believe I just stood there stiff as a stupid board trying to keep my distance from her, and from all of you." He took a deep breath. "Really, this has been the most amazing couple of days of my life. Next to seeing my kids born." His voice had tightened to a whisper. "I'll never forget this trip."

He regained his composure. "Honestly, I thought you were insane last night," he said, looking at Diane, "when you said you wanted me to tell the group about … well, you know …"

She held up her hand to pause him and asked the group, "How many of you were concerned when Jesse and I stayed back while you stepped onto the ice yesterday?" Every hand went up. "And what were you thinking?"

"I thought he was being difficult again," Rob said.

Marty said, "I didn't know what to think, but I could tell something had happened when you rejoined the group, though I couldn't tell what. I was kind of afraid to look at either of you, because I didn't want to get drawn into whatever it was and miss out on what was happening on the glacier."

Diane continued. "See, it's going on all the time, even when we aren't talking about it. You're always sensing what's going on under the surface and it's always affecting how steady and grounded you are. Whether you know it or not, your unspoken fears and how you unconsciously act them out are affecting you and everyone else. It's an underground feedback loop. I know some of you are thinking there's no time for this in the real world, but I'm telling you there is and that it pays to make the time to pause when something is going on and address it so you don't keep getting derailed.

"Most of you haven't seen enough of it to believe all of what I'm telling you. So far, you've seen how it played out in this deal with Marty. And, Jim, you've been experiencing some of it in the two deals we're working on together right now. Keep doing what you need to do to be the open, transparent, trusting and trustworthy guy in every transaction, Jim. Sure, not everyone is going to be like that. But keep selecting clients and partners, like Rob and Dan and Andrew, who also want to be that way. I promise you, as you do more of it with that kind of people, the cost of doing business with the other kind of people will reveal itself to be way too high to stomach. The people in this room aren't the only good people out there.

They are entrusting their life's work to us

"At the risk of sounding like a Pollyanna," Diane continued, "that's what I'm on a mission to do. Instead of continuing to allow ourselves to devolve to the lowest common denominator of dishonesty, deceit and deception, harming each other and terrorizing sellers in the process, I *know* we can shut those creatures down, make them ashamed of how they pollute the process and isolate them out of what have always been the noble professions we're engaged in.

"I never forget that the people who have spent their lives building their businesses entrust them to us—the professionals in this room—to help them to find their next owners, ones who will care for what they have built and help move them to the next level, and not at the expense of the humanity of the founders or each other. I decided long ago that I was going to keep looking for other professionals who cared about these business owners the way I do, but who needed support and encouragement to safely shepherd them through the sale process with respect and dignity and care, to gently place them on the other side, enriched not only with the financial rewards of what they spent their lives building, but with their spirits intact and their hearts ready to step into the next chapters of their lives.

"I refuse to participate in an industry in a way that strips owners of their dignity and leaves them shaken and scared, regretting that they sold their businesses. Too many of the millions of business owners who should be preparing to exit their companies have been traumatized by the stories of what has happened to others who have sold, and are going to die at their desks instead, harming their families and their communities in the process, because they think that's what will happen to them if they sell. And I'm not willing to let it continue. Those who continue to do it that way should be exposed for the thieves and spirit murderers they are. You," she indicated the people in the room, "shouldn't be ashamed and afraid that they'll take advantage of you and you shouldn't stoop to their cowardly, lying, brutal, toxic ways. *They* should be afraid of dignified, caring professionals like you, who will call out their tactics and leave them exposed and isolated. There is a better way."

Diane realized she was a little breathless and had grown perhaps over-emphatic with her last verbal missive.

"Oh, just that, huh, Diane? And here I thought you were planning to do something meaningful with your life," smirked Jesse, as the others laughed.

⋀ Not Out of the Woods Yet

"Alrighty, then!" said Dan, slapping his hands against his thighs and hoisting himself to his feet. "Shall we get a move on?"

Liza said, "Yes, we're gonna make our way down the trail in a few minutes, but before we go, a couple of things."

"First, I want to apologize for making decisions without involving you. Sometimes, as a guide, I can get caught up in being the guardian of everyone's safety. This has been a great reminder for me that sharing information and seeking input is the way I actually want to run my business. I don't have to pretend I always know the right way and I'm sorry for the way I contributed to yesterday's undercurrent."

Turning to Marty, she said, "I hope you know, Marty, that I'm not explaining away the choices I made and that I'm learning, too. I just wanted you to have the most wonderful day on the glacier that I could possibly make for you." He was beaming and reached for Liza's hand. "I am honored that you allowed me to help make your dream come true and to be with all of you," she indicated the others with a sweep of her hand, "to mark this new path in your journey."

Marty pulled her into a bear hug, "Aww, c'mere, kid. It was all I had hoped for and more." Patting her back as he let go, he said, "We're all learning, Liza, and yesterday, in fact every bit of this, is something I'll never forget."

Clearing her throat and tucking a lock of hair back under her cap to give her emotions a chance to subside, Liza said, "Second, the talk Diane just gave has another special application for us.

We won't exactly be able to see everything that's under our feet, under the snow, as we make our way down, especially for the first part, and then it's likely to be slick when we do get below the snowy parts. So, while it would be easy to become lax and think 'oh it's all downhill,' please remember that it's not over until we're all safely at the lodge for the night, OK?

We're all responsible for ourselves *and* each other

"Slow and steady is the name of the game. Use your poles; take your time. Make sure your footing is secure and leave a little room between each other, just in case. If one of you takes a tumble, we don't want everyone to fall like a line of dominoes. But also be alert to each other and your surroundings. We're all responsible for ourselves *and* each other. If you notice someone needs a break, call for it. Even if you feel frustrated and wish we could press on, we stay together." She paused. Normally, she wouldn't say this next part, but given what they'd just processed, she knew she needed to; otherwise, they'd all sense her heightened vigilance on the trail.

"Finally, remember we're in grizzly country. And right now, they're trying to eat as much and as fast as they can to prepare for hibernation, which means they're not as alert to our presence as they might be, especially with the fresh snow they have to dig through. All along the trail are huckleberry bushes, which are high-calorie treats for them. And today there will have been no other hikers to make noise to scare them off. It's our job to be alert for them. The same rules apply as I told you before we came up: if you see one, do *not* approach and do *not* run. Staying in a group is our best safety."

"Well, I know I don't have to outrun the bear," said Jesse, "I just have to outrun Rob and Marty!" There was some nervous laughter, but everyone knew it was no laughing matter if they actually did run into a bear.

Jim thought, "Well, isn't this *just* like every deal I've ever done: just when I thought we were out of the woods …"

Luckily, the snow wasn't quite as deep at the beginning of the trail as they thought it would be.

Andrew was a bit nervous about the possibility of running into a bear. Snapping branches made him blurt, "What was that?!" and he was increasingly testy as Jim kept unconsciously creeping up on him, just because his stride was longer and he was used to hiking faster. Truth be told, Liza was right, he *was* feeling impatient and *did* want to move the others along faster. He was frustrated with having to stop so often, especially when he could have made it in much less time on his own.

At one point, Diane whispered to him, "Jim, take a breath for heaven's sake. Look around. You're missing the view." When Jim looked up, he realized they were just above a break in the trees. When he looked out, he could see the entire valley spread out below.

He was the first to spot the movement in the woods to their right. Instinctively, he said, "Shh, look" and pointed. As he did a bighorn sheep trotted onto the path not fifteen feet in front of them. It was a mature ram, easily 300 pounds, his horns curled full circle. The animal lowered his head and widened his stance, clearly ready to defend—or charge. "Just stay still," Liza said quietly. Everyone stood perfectly still, frozen with fear and wonder. After a moment, the animal snorted and raised his head. He sniffed the air, watched them a little longer and then loped up the slope and out of view. None of them, except Liza, had ever been this close to something this wild.

Once they began breathing again, the group talked excitedly about what they had just seen. When they continued downhill, Marty noticed Andrew's continued nervousness. His off-key baritone sang out, "Feee-lingggs, nothin' wrong with feee-lingggs" to the groans of the others. "That's not how it goes, Marty!" "God help us!" and "At least we know there's no bears in the area now!"

Liza had estimated the time they'd needed for the trip back to the visitors' center, and she had asked Marius to radio for a driver to bring the van to meet them so they didn't have to wait for the hikers' shuttle.

As they were settling into the van for the ride to the lodge, and their last night together, Liza, sitting beside the driver, said, "Hey Jesse, this is your phone, right?" She handed it to Rob in the middle row to pass back to him. "I asked the staff to charge it and send it with the driver, in case you wanted it."

He took it and reflexively hit the on button but, thinking better of it, said, "I'll call my wife when we get settled in. But thanks. I think I'm just gonna enjoy the scenery. Who knows when I'll get back here." There were some smiles and raised eyebrows, but mostly everyone was thinking the same thing. The views were spectacular, and none of them really felt like diving into the real world just yet.

Just as on the drive several mornings ago, light snoring and bits of quiet conversation filled the drive along Going-to-the-Sun Road. It was a marvel, realizing that just a little more than a hundred years ago, almost no one would have been able to see all of this. Marty felt proud that they had made the trek to see the glaciers and, hearing that something was happening geologically made him even more grateful that they had experienced something so special.

Soon enough, the van pulled up in front of Lake McDonald Lodge. Those who were awake nudged those who were dozing, saying "We're here." Groggy eyes took in the changed scene as they climbed out of the van.

"I'm beat!" said Jim, stretching his long arms and legs. "I can't wait to get these boots off."

"I could use a shower," said Rob, "and so can you," ribbing Dan, who smiled an acknowledgment of that truth.

They pulled their day packs from the back of the van and stiffly followed Liza into the lobby, where she was gathering keys from the bellman. "Your luggage has already been taken to your rooms," she said, handing out keys.

"What's the plan?" asked Andrew.

"You've got a couple of hours to shower, take a nap, check your email, wander the grounds or take a walk down to the lake, if you want to stretch a little bit. We're gonna do dinner a bit earlier tonight, because there's a narrated slideshow over at the campground about the original construction of the roads and some of the early buildings. Marty and I thought it might be something you might like to see. It puts into perspective what you've experienced and gives you a glimpse of the parts of the park we didn't see. Kind of a capper on the trip. It starts at seven and is just a short walk from here. So, dinner here in the dining room at 5:30?"

The weary hikers wandered off down the hall to their rooms, grateful for not having to walk farther.

⋀ Willing to Walk Through Fire

They had decided on an informal dinner in the lodge's dining room, since at this time of year the dining room was sparsely populated because most of the tourists had already left the park. Diane planned to use this dinner as a bridge between what they had experienced together in the backcountry and preparing them for re-entry to the other parts of their lives. This was, in essence, a fork in the road of their shared journey.

They ordered and then engaged in easy banter, the stories already becoming gently embellished, speckled with anecdotes that helped to lock the memories in place with laughter. The chatter subsided as they tucked into steaks, fresh fish and still-warm bread.

As wine glasses were refilled, Diane asked if they were open to creating a kind of closing together. They turned their attention to her. "First, I'd like to thank Marty, our gracious host, for his kindness in including all of us in marking this changing path with him." She raised her glass. Marty was unaccustomed to being in the spotlight this way, but he met their eyes with brightness and took in their affection and respect. Everyone could feel the beginning of the shift, what Diane had called a transition time.

Then she said, "Liza, thank you for guiding us safely through the hills and valleys of a journey that will linger in our memories for the rest of our lives." Liza smiled at her friend, taking in the appreciation of those she had spent the past several days with.

"Marty," Diane asked, "may I open the floor to anyone who would like to share something about their experience before your closing words?" Marty bowed his head briefly to show his agreement.

"I'll go," said Dan. The others looked surprised. Dan had been the least talkative of them on the trip. "It was a complete surprise, Marty, when that invitation arrived in April. I remembered you saying

> This deal has been so much more than business

something about glaciers when we were at the closing dinner last year but I thought it was just the liquor-fueled enthusiasm of a seller relieved to have it all over and done. There was no way I could have envisioned how close we've become this past year, closer than I've been to any other owner I've worked with in the twenty years I've been in this business. It's been business, but it's been so much more.

"This trip allowed me to see more of the man who poured his acumen into his company, but his heart into his people. I couldn't be more thrilled to have been asked to join you on this trip. The selfish part of me would like to find a way to rope you into staying on, but the better part of me wishes you well as you and Marjorie discover new roads together.

"One more thing," Dan continued. "Jesse," he said, turning toward him, "when Marty told me he wanted to ask you to come along, I had hoped you would say yes. Mostly because I wanted you to see how well you and your company would fit with what Marty and I had built, but also because I wanted to spend some time getting to know you. It took balls for you to get real with us about your struggle. I know you were worried that it would make you vulnerable and that we might use it to take advantage of you. That made it all the more courageous for you to take the risk. It pulled away the mask that made you seem like a scared kid pretending he was in charge of a successful company. It made me respect you more.

"Marty and I talked about it and we want you in, just as much as we did before this trip, but now we're even clearer about why you fit with us. Diane talked about it yesterday—no, wait, was it this morning? Man, the days are a jumble. Anyway, we don't work with jerks—it's our no-asshole policy. As a firm, we call out that kind of crap when we see it. The reason we're able to build the kind of businesses we do is that we strip away that pretense and that means getting real, and yes, sometimes raw with each other. You did that last night.

"You don't have to make your decision tonight, Jesse. In fact, this trip was never about closing the deal with you. I told you we weren't here to talk business, we came to celebrate with our friend," Dan said, nodding toward Marty. "You said you weren't sure if you fit in, but these past couple of days, I'd say you walked the walk as well as any of us. And Marty and I are ready to walk an even rougher road with you. If that means Marty backs you up while you're doing chemo or recovering from surgery, we've got you. If you want it. And even if you decide not to join us, we've still got you.

"So, what did I learn? And how will it change the way I walk my own path? Strength comes from being willing to walk beside someone through fire, not from overpowering them. It's clear to me that the only path worth walking is with those who have your back. " Dan sat back down. Jesse's head was down, his eyes squeezed shut.

Jim went next, gripping Marty's shoulder as he stood. "Well, Dan pretty much stole my words. Marty, I too was shocked when the invitation arrived. I've never stayed in touch with another client after a deal closed but you showed me that the relationship is the part of what I do that I value most. The deal is an incidental part when I stay focused on what's happening with the person going through it. Corny as I thought it was the first time I heard it, 'it's a transition, not a transaction' is entirely accurate. I don't think I'll ever see it the same way again and it has been my honor to walk alongside you through this.

"But, man, you've spoiled it now! I'm gonna use you as the gold standard to hold other clients up to." He turned to Jesse. "Would I be willing to cross a glacier and fight a bear, even if it's one called cancer, with this man to help him get safely to the end of the road? That's the question I'm now gonna be asking myself as I choose clients and deal partners." With that, Jim sat down.

"I guess that makes me next," said Rob. "Buddy, we've known each other for more years than either of us would like to say. And golf is really more my speed than dragging my old body through snow up to my knees," he said, "but this journey, the whole shebang, not just this hiking trip, helped me realize there's a lot going on under the surface in every deal I do. I've kinda joked for years that I'm part psychologist in any transaction"— with that, Jim nodded vigorously—"but a lot of this is really above my pay grade. I know enough to spot when someone's struggling, that's for sure. But I'm better off doing the part I do well, the lawyering, and getting help for my clients. I've watched clients struggle for years with the process of letting go of their businesses, and until I learned all of this, this better way, I hadn't really realized it's the same thing that keeps me practicing, long after my wife, and certainly my younger partners, would have had me stop. It's given me new respect for just how hard the process is and how the transition, not just the transaction, requires a delicate hand. Who knows—my wife might just get what she's been nagging me for; I might even start thinking about my own exit. But don't go spilling the beans, OK? I might need Diane to do that 'whispering' she does on me if I'm going to face those kinds of tough exit questions for myself."

Andrew opened his hand to Jesse, questioning, "You or me?" Jesse nodded for him to go. "OK. I've been the financial advisor for a lot of folks over the years, and I've heard a bunch of different ideas about what people think they're going to do when they finally sell their companies and retire. I've even received a good number of postcards from trips that actually happened, but I've never been invited to *go* on one of those trips. Marty, you're going to be a hard act to follow!"

Andrew reached across the table and refilled Jesse's wine glass. "I've learned a couple of things through all of this, and I'm sure there will be other lessons that filter up in the weeks to come, but I'll say this. It's not enough to just have a rough outline of what comes after the sale. I've been too lax in really diving in to understand what my clients meant by 'travel.' To be honest, I also never really understood the challenges that came with letting go of a business and how it can activate the same anxiety that happens when the kids leave home.

What's the money really for?

"It really helped to understand how lost an owner, or a couple, can feel as they approach the sale. So much emphasis is put on getting the money for them that I think all of us," he gestured at the other professionals around the table, "lose sight of what the business or the money might be standing in front of for either or both of them. Diane once described how many people actually grieve the spousal relationship that withered because all their energy was directed toward kids or the business. I've seen it in my own marriage, but I didn't have a name for it. I just thought my clients were being stubborn, holding onto a business thinking they wanted more money. I hadn't thought about how devastated they might be to face what was staring them in the face when that was no longer a distraction. Or how much like a bottomless ice hole it might feel like, facing days stretching before them without the safety harness the business routine had provided."

Andrew looked toward Diane. "When you said we know how to prepare our kids to launch, but no one teaches us how to launch into what comes after work, I realized how true that is, and why people hate the word 'retirement.' It makes total sense to me now why clients say they'd rather die at their desk than retire. They don't see clearly what life will be after that.

"So, what will I do differently? I'll have my sensor up for when my clients are struggling with launching and letting go of their business and I'll see it as something that requires emotional support, not more charts showing the money picture. And, I'm not too proud to say I'm going to figure out how all of this is playing out in my relationship with my wife and kids, and maybe even with my parents and my business partners." Someone thumped the table in agreement as Andrew sat down.

"I guess that leaves me," said Jesse. "I can tell you, I've heard a lot said out loud this week that I've only ever thought. Certainly from my own mouth, but also from each of you. I understand now why I was always worried that someone else was hiding something from me: I was often playing hide-the-ball myself. And I'm not proud of that, let me tell you. But I didn't know there was another way. I always figured that any banker or broker who approached me to sell my business was in it for themselves and that I'd have to be on my guard to make sure I was getting everything I was owed. I lawyered up and was prepared to fight with Dan and Marty and whoever else I needed to.

"I came into this process wondering if I'd be able to bite my tongue and stick around long enough to get my earn-out if I sold, thinking it was just what I'd have to do to make sure I didn't get screwed. It hadn't occurred to me that I might enjoy that time or that it was how I'd get actual support in taking the company beyond what I could do on my own. It was beyond anything I could have thought, the idea that I might find partners I could trust, and let my guard down.

"I've been dancing in and out of this process over the past couple of months, thinking I'd sell and then pulling back, thinking maybe I'll run it on my own for another year and see if I could get an even higher multiple. That's where I was a couple of weeks ago. Dan, you were right, I was pulling away. And I couldn't make sense of it—you didn't chase me like the other guys my banker brought to me were doing. In fact, my lawyer and the banker were pressing me even harder to sign with one of those guys who were all over me. It seemed like all they wanted was for me to sign what they put in front of me and get it over with so they could get their money and move on to something else.

"Then, when they told me about the cancer, I got scared. Scared about selling, scared about not selling. I felt even more trapped and figured I'd have to do it on my own. There was no way I was going to tell any of this to any of you when I walked into that lodge that first night. And I wasn't even sure I had enough guts to say it last night when Diane asked me to. But I thought, what the hell did I have to lose?" Jesse paused to take a couple of deep breaths.

"No one, and I mean *no one*, has ever stepped up for me the way you guys did last night. And stupid as it sounds—and I felt like crap when I got up off that floor this morning—it meant everything to me last night to know I wasn't alone, even though the damn lizard wanted me to run out into the snow and pretend I hadn't said everything I did. But I stayed. Every one of you stayed. And then I wasn't quite as scared. I've never really asked for help before, but now I've come up against something where I'm going to have to ask for help. I didn't know it before, but that was exactly where I was about selling my business, too; I just couldn't see it because I was so busy pretending I didn't need help. I guess that's the good part about this. I didn't know that if I asked for help, someone would be there who wasn't going to rip me off.

"Marty, this trip was about you. Celebrating the great business you built and what you and Dan have done in the past year to make it even better. I've never heard of anyone doing something like this—celebrating a year later and keeping in touch with the people who helped you. I don't know how you came up with this idea, but if I make it a whole year, I want to do something like this, too. Something epic.

"I'm so sad that your accountant—is it Karen?—couldn't come on this trip. It's kind of cosmic that she's with someone who is dying and that's how I got to come, given what's happening for me now. I just want to thank you for giving me this chance to see this amazing place, but also to see a completely different way to look at selling my business and what it can mean for me and my family. It sounds dorky, but I want to grow up to be just like you. It would sure be something to feel as happy as you are after selling your business, and to see how many people care about you. It sure isn't how I hear other people talk about it."

"Marty, last words?" asked Diane.

"Let me start by saying how truly honored I am that each of you was willing to put aside your work and your family to come on this adventure with me. It means more to me than you could imagine. Jesse, I'd never heard of such a thing either—keeping in touch, celebrating a year later. Every poor schmuck I'd ever heard talk about selling gave the impression they'd barely escaped with their skin intact. They talked about it like something they wouldn't recommend to their worst enemy, let alone their friends. That's the direction I was headed, too. As everyone here knows, I was on a disaster course, pulling out all the stops trying to get out of selling the damned thing, because it all felt out of control and I had no idea what the other side would look like, except for the big pile of cash. And even that didn't feel like it was going to cushion my fall.

It meant everything to know I wasn't alone

"I had no idea who I was without my business, or what I was going to do with myself. Sure, I told Andrew, and everyone else, that I was going to golf and travel. I even blabbed on about buying a boat and sailing the world. It sounded like what a successful big shot who'd made a lot of money would do. Never mind that I had no idea what that even looked like, not to mention that Marjorie wasn't going to be part of that picture. I just needed to not let anyone know I was terrified and had no idea what I was doing.

"Truth? I should have sold the business five years ago and it's only because I got lucky with the way the market was that we lasted that long. I was worn out and the business had been coasting for years. I couldn't have done alone what Dan and I have done together. I only got reinvigorated once we got in there together.

"At the time of the sale, I was scared that I'd only have a year to figure all this stuff out before I'd have to leave. Honestly,

I was secretly hoping he'd still need me and I wouldn't have to actually leave when my year was up. Not because I loved it so much, or even had that much energy left to give it. When I'm honest, although I'd have never admitted this before, it was because it was the only thing I knew and I had no idea what my life would be like without it. That's not the case anymore. Would I stay if Dan asked me to? Only if Marjorie said I could," he joked. "Seriously, Jesse, if you join with Dan and you need me to help until you're back on your feet, of course I'll be there. But only because it means helping someone I care about, not because I can't let go. And because Dan will miss me."

I felt energized after completing the deal

Dan was smiling and nodding. He would indeed miss his days with Marty, but he figured they'd likely still see each other—just not like some other former CEOs who kept hanging around like homeless puppies.

"As for you guys," Marty continued, looking at Jim and Rob and Andrew, "I had this crazy conversation with Diane one day about the fact that I'd spent so much time with all of you during the deal that I'd kinda miss you. She said, 'Why don't you tell them?' I said 'What? Like say, Can I still hang out with you even after the deal is over?' None of you who've gotten to know her will be surprised that she said, 'Yeah, just like that!'" They all laughed, because that was exactly what Diane would say.

"Well, I wasn't quite there yet. But to paraphrase, 'I've come a long way, baby!' She had given me this task, to think about something to look forward to as I made my way through the year with Dan. At the time, I was still thinking that it was going to be a slog. To, as Jesse put it, make sure Dan didn't screw me out of my final pay-out."

Dan held up his hands, "Wait a second, does *everyone* think I'm out to screw them? C'mon, I'm actually a good guy!"

"Yeah, you are, Dan, but you're an investor and those guys have a bad rep; you know that. And I didn't know you then like I know you now. Anyway," Marty continued, "I started talking about this picture of the glaciers I'd seen as a kid. It turned into my vision, what I wanted to do when I finally got out from under Dan's thumb," he said, just ribbing. "But then I started realizing how really different all of this was. Not just Dan and how great things were working with him. But how clear it was that we were doing something not at all like what so many others who had sold their businesses had done. But also, how different the process had been. How Jim had turned things around when he reached out to Diane when I went off the deep end. And how Rob and Dan's lawyer had worked together differently than they had before everything came unraveled. How including Karen and Andrew, and even Marjorie, in the process had made a difference.

"Instead of feeling worn out and beaten up at the end of the deal, I was actually *happy*! Not happy it was over, but happy with how things had gone. I felt respected and I felt that same respect for each of you. I wasn't kidding when I told Diane I would actually miss spending time with you. Who sells their company and then says they miss their lawyer? No offense, Rob. Or that they miss seeing their banker's name come up on their phone? But that was me."

"Lots of people had warned me that I'd feel seller's remorse after the deal. But I didn't. I felt proud of what we'd done together. And, well, I guess that's what led to this trip. Sure, it was something I wanted to do to celebrate, to mark the end of the year, the commitment I'd made to Dan when he bought my company. But I didn't make all of that happen on my own. It happened because of all of you and the way you embraced a way of doing this deal that was different, really different, than the way most deals get done. Kinder. More humane. You left me feeling cared for, and as Diane said this morning, safely landed on the other shore.

I was happy I sold my business

"So, my friends, before we head over to the campground to watch how all of this beauty around us was made, a toast: To all of you," he lifted his glass, and so did they, "for accompanying me on both legs of this challenging journey. May your journeys tomorrow to your homes be safe, and may you carry with you the memories we have made together. Take good care of our friend Jesse, and all the other travelers you meet along this path who are yet to come."

About the Author

Denise Logan knows that to business owners, selling a business is more than a transaction. To them, it is an emotionally fraught period of transition, filled with unexpected highs and lows, with no clear vision of what waits at the end for them and their family. Her passion for this work is colored by her own experience of being an unprepared business owner who made an abrupt and choppy exit from her company, after ignoring the signs that it was time for several years.

Her exit was followed by several years traveling in a 36-foot motorhome all over North and Central America, on her own, with two sweet little dogs, but that's a story for another book.

Weaving together her background as a lawyer, social worker and business owner has enabled Denise to walk alongside hundreds of business owners and their professional teams to ease the emotional process of transition as they navigate the complex world of selling their business and letting go into their own version of what's next.

Her work as The Seller Whisperer™ frees up professional advisors to focus on the transactional work they do best while ensuring that the business owner has the kind of emotional support from a right-brain-thinking partner to make it all the way through a successful close, enhancing the likelihood of a successful conclusion and keeping costs in check and delays to a minimum.

Since founding Chase What Matters in 2010, Denise has spoken to audiences on three continents and is a frequent commentator on the subjects of business succession planning, transition and legacy. She has also provided advanced training to advisors employed by some of the world's largest financial institutions, law firms and accounting firms, helping their clients successfully transition their businesses to new owners.

Born in Ontario, Canada, but educated in the United States, she now lives in Arizona, where she is happy to remind others when it's hot that they don't have to shovel sunshine.

Public Speaking

One of the least expected but most rewarding experiences during the writing of this book has been the opportunity to travel extensively and speak to business owners and their trusted advisors about the personal and professional experiences that led me to write *The Seller's Journey*.

Most of my speeches have been organized by attorneys, accountants, wealth management professionals, merger and acquisition firms, financial services firms, investment banks, business brokers, industry associations and private equity firms. If you own a business, or advise business owners, and want to learn more about booking me to speak, or to order additional copies of *The Seller's Journey* to share with your clients, please visit

www.TheSellersJourney.com